POWERHOUSE
WOMEN
Survivor **TO** *Thriver*

PRESENTED BY

 NYX PUBLISHING

First published in 2021 by Onyx Publishing, an imprint of Notebook Publishing of Notebook Group Limited, 20–22 Wenlock Road, London, N1 7GU.

www.onyxpublishing.com

ISBN: 9781913206574

A CIP catalogue record for this book is available from the British Library.

Typeset by Onyx Publishing of Notebook Group Limited.

To all the Powerhouse Women who have made the brave decision not to fall victim to circumstance, but rather to thrive in the wake of trauma.

Your strength is a beacon in the darkness.

You are inspiring.

CONTENTS

FOREWORD

It never fails to surprise me quite how empowering and awe-inspiring women can be...

Within these pages, you will be introduced to some of the most incredible women who, despite experiencing a vast array of trauma, pain, hardship and tragedy, have each made a very conscious decision not to view themselves and their world through the lens of victimhood, but rather to build the most beautiful life, regardless of the rubble of the past.

The unwavering focus on gratitude and the appreciation for life and all it has to offer—irrespective of the character-shaping moments that have brought unexpected weathers and choppy seas—are truly inspirational. The continuous determination and drive to keep pushing forward, to never settle for less than and to actively strive for more, is a perspective that shows the way like a hope-inspiring lighthouse, not only for when times get a little darker, but for when those still navigating stormy waters need to know safety isn't too far away.

Without question, it takes resilience and strength to move through trauma and decide to thrive despite it all, and that is something each and every one of the contributing authors in this book have done—and not just once, but as a constant behaviour, every single day.

What's so important to recognize is that all of us, every single one of us, regardless of background or what we've been led to believe about ourselves and the world around us, is capable of amazing things. There is only one person that ever needs convincing that we can, in fact, thrive in the wake of trauma—and that's ourselves.

As soon as we start to believe and do the work, moving out of a place of fear and into a space of power, we become truly untouchable—and that's where the magic begins to come to life.

So, to all the Powerhouse Women who have brushed themselves down and chosen not to merely survive but to thrive despite it all, you're amazing. You're an example of what can be if only you decide.

Hayley Paige
Domestic Violence Survivor and Campaigner, and Founder & CEO of Onyx Publishing

ALEISHA BECKUM

Non-Profit Accounting & Grants Management Expert, Positively Impacting the Lives of Our Communities

ONCE UPON A TIME, there was a little girl named Aleisha who, at the age of six, only knew chaos: she was exposed to a life in which she constantly witnessed her father's abuse of her mother—a mother who then became fed up with the abuse and so dragged Aleisha and her younger siblings from California to Arkansas, away from all the family she knew, to a place filled with the unknown.

Aleisha was also almost immediately exposed to abuse in the form of molestation by the man her mother would marry. Between the ages of six and eight, she endured, daily, the horror that is molestation by the hands of this man she didn't know. He would make his attempts every night when she would sleep, and would sometimes even do so in plain sight, under the covers in the living room, while her family was around.

At the age of eight, Aleisha realized this was not normal behavior, and so she did everything she could to prevent his heinous acts. Having become an extremely light sleeper due to his nightly attempts, she developed survival habits that would allow her to predict his every move.

Now, one may wonder, *Why didn't she say anything?*, but when one grows up in a household where all family is mentally absent, ignoring these acts as they are carried out before their very eyes, you often find that you don't have anyone to turn to about what is happening. No; the only thing running through your mind at this point is survival, plain and simple.

Time went on, and, as if nothing was happening, the little girl began to assume the role of a mother to her younger siblings. She grew up too fast, experiencing no childhood whatsoever—and yet, at eight years old, she knew she was going to make something of her life so she could escape one day; *that* was her sole focus.

Meanwhile, her extended family in California knew of Aleisha's duties within the household and occasionally mentioned that she shouldn't be carrying the burden of such "motherly" things—and yet no one actually confronted her mother. Having had all her family turn a blind eye to her hardships, Aleisha felt even more unsafe. It dawned on her that she only had herself to rely on.

She journaled every day—her outlet for what she was dealing with—and with these entries, time continued to go on, the man continuing to make every attempt to touch her or watch her somehow all the while. This became a normal part of her day for her. However, it didn't stop there: slowly but surely, attempts started to be made by other men within the family, as well as men brought in by family members.

By the time she was thirteen, Aleisha had endured much molestation from other men, as well as other various inappropriate sexual advances. When reflecting on her childhood now, she finds she has no recollection of a single memory with her mother, or really as a family: the little girl was the one to initiate "family dinners". There was a "kids' living room" and "parents' living room", meaning the children had little to no daily interaction with their mother. Overall, life felt like a giant blur of nothingness.

One summer, after returning from visiting her father, Aleisha found her bedroom to have been completely redone from top to bottom. Her mother's husband told her he had done it for her so that she had a big mirror that she could get ready in. It wasn't until later that year that her little sister heard kittens meowing from the other side of the closet. The little sister went under the house and into the other side of the closet and mentioned to Aleisha that she could see inside Aleisha's bathroom and bedroom from it. Further investigation by Aleisha and her sister did, indeed, prove that her mother's husband had not upgraded her room out of the kindness of his heart; rather, he had done so to enable him to spy on her through a two-way mirror into the bathroom and bedroom.

She was absolutely mortified as she thought back to all the times he must have seen her naked—amongst other things. From that point forward, she did everything in the dark—showered in the dark; got dressed in the dark—for fear he would be able to see her.

She was now fourteen—a pivotal moment in her life; one that would set her on the trajectory that would lead her to where she is today.

One day, after coming home from school, Aleisha was talking to her boyfriend at the time on the phone when she overheard her mother yelling. Of course, she started to panic, and, as she listened to her mother, it seemed that her mother had found out about her husband doing inappropriate things to Aleisha—a conclusion Aleisha came to after hearing mention of him wrongfully recording someone (something Aleisha had secretly suspected him of doing for some time).

Aleisha started to cry, not knowing what was going to happen now.

It was at that moment that Aleisha's mother came into Aleisha's room and immediately asked, "Why are you crying?"

"Nothing."

Her mother pried, and, suddenly incredibly overwhelmed, Aleisha spilled everything, from the molestations to the two-way mirror.

Her mother's response was to question her as though she was lying. "Are you sure it was him?' Then, "You're going to tell him everything you just told me."

Suddenly, everyone was in Aleisha's room, her mother looking down at Aleisha and her husband while they both sat on the edge of Aleisha's bed.

"Tell him what you have just told me," she ordered Aleisha.

"You know what you've done," Aleisha said to him.

He paused. "I'm sorry."

Aleisha's mother pressed on, "Do you think you can ever forgive him and feel safe here?"

"I don't know."

"What do you need to feel safe?"

Aleisha thought for a moment. "The mirror needs to be fixed."

After that conversation, he was kicked out of the

house for two weeks before being let back in. The entire family knew what had happened, but no one did anything; no one protected Aleisha. They just kept asking if she was doing okay.

By the time Aleisha turned fifteen, she had been raped by the husband's sister's boyfriend. Again, no one did anything.

Aleisha became a very angry person. She was entirely alone and felt abandoned. She would later run away to her dad in Sacramento, CA, who had had no idea she was coming. She would tell him everything that had happened, and CPS would immediately get involved, leading to her mother's husband going to prison. Her mother would also follow suit soon thereafter. As a result, the entire family was broken up in the blink of an eye.

Her father took her in and provided a home and stability for the remainder of her high school years by getting her into sports and giving her a routine, in turn helping her to rebuild her self-esteem. He also had her go to counseling—a tremendous help since it allowed her to process the things that she had suppressed from being six years old. Indeed, it was through this counselling that she began to realize that she didn't have the slightest clue about how to properly and effectively communicate her needs, boundaries, and wants. As a result, she would continue to go to counseling for several years, doing

EMDR work and finding ways to see life in brighter colors again—much like when you are a child; when life hasn't yet had the chance to put its grip around you.

Who Aleisha was versus who I am today are two completely different people: I am no longer afraid to speak up and I will never allow someone to take advantage of me ever again. The rage I felt inside fueled my obsession to succeed and achieve as much as I possibly can; to create a life without chaos, filled with love and freedom.

I also knew from the age of sixteen that I wanted to have my own business—and, in turn, I would attend Sacramento State University, join a sorority and co-ed business fraternity, take seven courses each semester to ensure I graduated within four years, and take care of my younger brother (who my dad was unable to take care of since he didn't know how to juggle childcare with working thirty-two hours a week while living on his own).

I also had a boyfriend at the time, who I am grateful for, since his family provided a sense of stability and normalcy in my life, which would only reinforce the feeling of safety—no chaos—and success I wanted for myself.

Throughout those years of attending college and working as a student for the State of California, I bounced around a lot with various state jobs, only lasting about a year (if that) in each. I bounced around so much because I would easily get bored of what I was doing: I have ADHD and a very Type A personality, meaning I would quickly learn everything and then would want to learn something else. Each year, I would make $5k–$10k more than the year before by elevating myself at each new job, never staying complacent with where I was. I was often identified as being "insatiable". I also had a shopping addiction, buying things I wasn't able to afford to pay back on time, only making minimum payments. I acquired a lot of unnecessary consumer debt in the process, but then again, I'd had no guidance; no one to look up to or help me. I made a lot of poor financial decisions around that time, and I never saved my money because my mindset was, *Well, I could die tomorrow, and I can't take this money with me.*

I graduated college and shortly thereafter broke up with my boyfriend. I then had the task of finding a permanent job: my contract with the state was ending after graduation. I had no car or savings, and I was unable to find a job within three months of my contract that would be able to support me. In the end, I had to file for unemployment. As a result, I quickly found I was unable to afford where my brother and I were living. I had also accumulated almost $18k worth of credit card debt, meaning I had to begin selling everything in the house just to make ends meet.

This was one of the lowest points in my life financially. I had to tell my brother that he needed to try and work things out with our dad so he could go back and live with him, as I couldn't afford to take care of him anymore.

I would later move into a house that I shared with four other strangers since my rent would then be $325 instead of $800—something that worked well, considering my unemployment was $1,000 a month.

I would later land a job working for the State of California again, as an auditor this time. My job was to audit cities and counties throughout the state, and while working there, I gained a tremendous amount of knowledge. However, I also became exposed to the corruption that prevails within the state—and when I tried to expose this, they told me to stop. At my insistence, I was threatened with termination.

Termination? I hadn't done anything wrong! Indeed, I was set up—not only for not listening to them with regards staying quiet about what they were doing, but also for not caving to my supervisor's sexual advances. I was put on administrative leave for about a month and, when I returned, I received a large packet of information they had compiled against me. However, they were far from the smartest: they essentially put themselves in the firing line by providing the documentation themselves, meaning I didn't even have to prove myself in the end.

Long story short, my supervisor was fired, and I was told that they would drop everything so long as I went and found another job.

Ultimately, this was the catalyst that led me to pursue my current career path—a blessing in disguise.

I finally got out of working in government and went into the private sector, finding a job as a consultant to prepare what I had been auditing for the state. What a coincidence! I hadn't even known this was a thing; I'd never paid attention to the companies that prepared the reports I audited, since I'd assumed that the city or county themselves prepared it. Lo and behold, other companies actually do this! I just so happened to find a company that would prepare these reports for cities and counties located only five miles from me. This instilled so much excitement for me: now, I could potentially make a change from the outside!

I really enjoyed the work I was doing, but it only lasted for about two years: the company was experiencing financial struggles, and that worried me. Hence, I left to join an accounting firm I knew I could grow into. Within three months of working there, the owner presented the offer that I take over the company. I was truly flattered—and yet, as I dove deeper into my job, I realized that working with for-profit companies was not what I was passionate about: I didn't care about taking over a company within the next five years that I had only been working at for seven months. Regardless, the owner of the company gave me something even more special than this offer: confidence that I could have a company of my own.

Encouraged by this seal of trust, I started my own business on the side in 2017 to provide consulting services to cities/counties and non-profits in accounting and grants management, which included consulting the reports that I used to audit and providing web design services to various companies.

All the while, I was enjoying my life with my then-boyfriend, who I had been with for eight years. We dealt with a lot of trust issues, among other things, that he had created in the relationship. However, what he did do right was help me on the path of creating a business and show me how to navigate the space so that I didn't fall on my face. He also got me started in drag racing in early 2018. I had never raced before, but in just one year, I was racing faster than most of the guys in the industry. I would ultimately be featured on Discovery Channel's *Street Outlaws* and kick major butt!

I was conquering so much: I was making a name for myself in the racing community all across the country and in my own community, being asked to complete interviews and go on the radio, and was even invited to race all over the country. It was a thrill, and I am tremendously grateful for the opportunity he and others gave me. I felt like I was on top of the world: I was getting my company up and running, and drag racing almost every weekend all over the state.

I had always envisioned a life where I would continue to grow my business in consulting and web design services and be free from day-to-day life. I hated having to be at work by a certain time; I hated having to go to class in college; I hated only being able to take a thirty-minute or one-hour lunch break; I hated that I had to physically be at my desk, even though I had finished all of my work within a few hours of starting my day. I was never someone who wanted to be told what to do *ever*: I wanted to create my own schedule. I would often get in trouble at work for being late, taking longer lunches, and leaving early—and, in college, I would get in trouble for not attending lectures, which was what ultimately prompted me to take as many online courses as I could.

My point here? *I was not meant to fit into a box.* I was not meant to be told how to live my life—something that fueled my resolve to continue developing my business. This was very challenging, however: I had no idea what I was doing, but I went for it regardless. I only knew that I was resourceful and could figure anything out.

I started by understanding all of the foundational pieces that I needed, such as setting up a business bank account, obtaining an EIN, registering with the state, etc.

I realized during these moments that I didn't really have anyone to go to to help me with everything—not even my then-boyfriend, who was a successful entrepreneur. I think he thought highly of me and knew I would figure it out myself, but I also had a feeling that he didn't *truly* want me to be super-successful, since that would mean I wouldn't really need him at all. I would mention hiring a coach and he would tell me, "You have me to help you," but I didn't, which was odd.

Throughout my years—even today—my family has never supported me; they have only called for money or asked for me to hire them, not because they wanted to help but because they wanted to benefit from my work, too.

Indeed, I have felt very lonely and sad over the years—and to add insult to injury, not many women have wanted to be my friend. This makes me sad because I am a major empath and care deeply for others—too much, sometimes. Hence, it truly hurts my feelings when I don't really receive much support.

Building my business myself has had what feels like more downs than ups: while the business is sustainable, it has been a challenge to grow it the way I have wanted to in a timeframe I desire. I have paid to be part of various mentorship programs—one being an absolute scam and the other feeling pretty unrelatable to me, considering my space is very niche. I don't believe you can adopt a "cookie-cutter approach" when it comes to business, and that is what I felt was the case in my latest mentorship program: I felt like an outcast and like no one understood (or took the time to understand) what I was doing. Again, I didn't feel like I could truly receive the support, guidance, and advice that I need to put me on the trajectory for ultimate success.

My goal for success consists of various aspects, one of which is being able to help as many people as I can. I am a giver; a helper; an empath. It is my duty to help. My business uProfyt (You Profit) consists of providing financial and grants management services to nonprofit organizations: when the organizations have a strong financial foundation, they can make better strategic decisions, identify gaps, and maximize and recover funding that is being left on the table that would otherwise allow them to further carry out their mission by impacting more lives within our communities. As we know, nonprofits struggle for funding already, having to rely on donations, fundraisers, grants, etc., to make money so they can provide the programs our communities depend on—which is why it's so crucial that nonprofits are well-equipped to manage their organizations from a financial standpoint so they can stay afloat and carry out their mission. By serving nonprofits, we can serve the masses—and that is my way of giving back to the world at a larger scale: having a business with a purpose.

With the knowledge and expertise I have attained, I feel that it is my duty to be successful in uProfyt. The employees that join my team have a deep passion to help others, and they want to make a tangible, positive impact on our world.

My clients have been able to achieve incredible results through these services. I start with the accounting/financial stage to ensure they are complying with federal and state regulations and accounting for everything properly (but also, more importantly, in a way that will allow them to achieve maximum benefits); after all, if an organization is not aware of the ins and outs of regulations and how they can use them to their advantage, they are missing out on opportunities that could benefit them tremendously. With just one simple regulation, they could save thousands of dollars—a significant amount of money to not have to dish out and which can then be better utilized for more important and immediate needs for the organization!

Through this process alone, we have been able to help organizations to properly budget and recognize revenues accordingly—which has resulted in our bringing in well over one million dollars in additional revenues to some organizations by simply accounting for and budgeting everything properly.

With this next stage of understanding their true cost

of service, we prepare various reports called Cost Allocation Plans and Indirect Cost Rate Proposals, which identify how much it costs the organization as a whole and at a programmatic level. If they do not understand these costs, they are most certainly losing money unnecessarily, which can lead to the shutdown of an organization or the continual facing of financial hardships if not managed properly. Hence, if we think about the opportunity that exists for organizations to impact more lives, it makes sense that they understand first how much it even costs them to do so: if they know their financial goals of fundraising and obtaining grant funding, how many people to hire, where resources should be allocated to, etc., then they can better and more efficiently serve their mission from a strategic standpoint. This process has been able to bring in over one hundred million dollars in funding reimbursements to our clients, including state and local government organizations, which positively impacts us as taxpayers. Some of these recovered monies have been brought about due to something as simple as including just one line item cost in these reports.

One of our greatest services is one whereby we work with organizations who have already received grant funding and weren't able, in their mind, to recover the full grant amount. By preparing a Cost Allocation Plan and Indirect Cost Rate proposal, we can tap into those unspent funds, which can bring additional monies into the organization that they didn't even realize they could receive. This has resulted in our being able to recover over two million dollars in funding in such organizations. From there, they are then able to use those funds to again further impact the lives of their communities—which further carries out their mission!

The best bit? Our outgoings to provide such services are potentially zero, if done properly. With that in mind, this whole system is a complete no-brainer. uProfyt is paid via the provision of these amazing services, as the nonprofit organization receives expert knowledge and services to bring them greater financial stability and allow them to maximize their funding and impact more lives—all at zero cost to them.

In this way, our communities are better served at the capacity they deserve; it's a win-win-win for everyone! Together, we overcome; together, we win; together, we can change the world.

It feels incredible to be able to state that this is the mission of my company, because it's all I ever dreamed of as a child; coming together, supporting one another, changing the world—making it better. This just goes to prove that little Aleisha's vision was clear and achievable, regardless of the circumstances she found herself in, and I honestly think that's because she didn't give up, but decided to thrive in the wake of trauma.

Contact Aleisha

f www.facebook.com/beckumaleisha

⊛ www.uprofyt.com

in www.linkedin.com/in/aleishabeckum

📷 www.instagram.com/aleishabee

✉ abeckum@uprofyt.com

SHANÉ TERAN

Executive Wellness Coach, Psychotherapist, and OD Psychologist

MY LIFE STORY WAS predicted to end way before I made it home from the hospital as a newborn with my mother.

As an African American baby diagnosed with sickle cell disease, I had no clue that the words exchanged about my life at that time would haunt me into my adult life. My mom has told me the story time and time again: the doctors said that I wouldn't live long enough to reach adulthood; that, coupled with the short time I would have here on Earth, I would also be crippled by a developmental delay.

When telling this story to myself and others—especially after my attaining another accomplishment—my mother would tearfully proclaim that she knew better than to believe the doctors; besides, out of all six of her girls, I was the only one who managed to break her ribs during childbirth and give the nurses a purposefully cold stare within hours of my arrival.

Although I'm unable to recall the details from my own memories, I do remember having a very curated and constant fear that I would die—a fear that hijacked my childhood. At the time, it wasn't that I was suicidal in the very literal sense of wanting to kill or cause harm to myself, but there most definitely was an affixed dissonance between me and the world very early on. My sisters now tell me that they would often lift me onto their shoulders to triumphantly proclaim I was the *Queen of Sheba*—something I cannot remember amongst all the other memories of my being bedridden due to sickle cell pain "crises", unable to join them whenever they went out to play. It was like I was in a bubble and beyond imaginative play at that point: when I was inside, no one could (or seemed to know how to) do anything to help me feel less isolated.

What I *do* remember to be fun was playing around as

if I had my own business: I'd take old check ledgers and broken computer keyboards and "do business". The bathroom was the elevator, and I had an office on the top floor of the high-rise, of course!

Then, there was the Pentecostal-Apostolic preaching I heard weekly (but which felt like daily) from my dad's sermons, reminding us and the congregation that *we're living in the last days; God is going to rapture us up into the sky any day now; He'll come like a thief in the night, so be ready*—all of which I took very literally.

So, according to the doctors, I was not going to live for long because of my diagnosis—and, according to the Bible and my father, the Bishop of the church, I was going to leave this earth in the blink of an eye. Needless to say, "what's the point" quickly became my disposition as a result of this and the emotional, verbal, and physical abuse I experienced throughout my childhood. Staying busy and out of the way gave me some degree of solace during this time. Even still, the point of living didn't quite make sense to me—until one day, I looked up and realized I was eighteen years old, still alive, a straight-A student heading off to college, and away from home, in Cleveland, OH, for the first time.

As soon as I began to open up to the possibilities of a future, it was game on! I became a freshman resident advisor (RA) to third- and fourth-year college kids and slowly but surely started to become more and more aware of who I was and how I wanted to show up in the world.

However, not all was well in Paradise: rearing its serpent-like head, it was in my first English course within the first semester of my freshman year that I was told that I was a "pseudo-intellectual" by my white male English professor, who refused to grade my work. I was also soon discouraged from double-majoring in both social work and psychology by a white male department chair, who stated I "wouldn't be able to handle it".

Fast-forward to my entering a doctoral program while experiencing seemingly debilitating symptoms from a recent car collision-related traumatic brain injury (TBI), and my white female professor's comment that I was "not doctoral material" certainly came across as rather ludicrous—especially considering I was maintaining a 3.8 GPA despite the aforementioned intellectual, physical, and emotional challenges I was working through!

To be quite frank, I'd like to think that over the years, my passion turned into a need to prove everyone wrong—but in reality, I was instead fueled by my longer-than-expected life, the muscle memory of staying busy and out of the way, and the tug from my God-given purpose.

Here is another truth: I have incessantly dealt with residual effects from what people have said and done to try to break me down over the years. From such an extraordinary journey, I quickly became determined to help people become better human beings.

Just as I had been written off, I can't help but recall the time when my nephew limped into the dining room at three years old after being released from the local Emergency Department—the same age as my son at the time of this account—his stomach protruding from his already-malnourished frame, beaten nearly to death, eyes widened from the trauma, with who-knows-what type of messaging surging through his every fiber and emotional blueprint. From that moment on, I harbored a burning desire to figure out what could cause someone to intentionally try to break another person. Needless to say, passion for justice and finding the pieces to destructive cycles came alive within me and were added to the pot. I suddenly felt it necessary to establish who and what led to the hurt placed upon the many "victims" who had not yet found their paths to a state of thriving. I wasn't sure where this fire was going to lead me; this journey of finding, helping, and transforming those who were suffering.

After digging into a little research and taking time to explore the lives of leaders and influencers from around the world, I came to the realization that many leaders who genuinely wanted to help people weren't always aware of their own purpose or how to turn their own nightmares into envisioned service—so, instead of trying to kill or blot out the darkness that seemingly crippled so many on their paths, I thought I'd help people to see how much light they could shine into dark places. Not everybody is meant to be a leader or a healer, but that doesn't mean that everyone who's born to lead takes on that role with open arms from the get-go. We all have our stories, including the leaders and influencers of our generation; it's what we do with our stories that reflects either light or darkness into the world around us.

Despite finding what I believed to be my purpose, however, I kept second-guessing myself: how could it be that all of my trauma, both vicarious and first-hand, could have a direct impact on people for good? Who would ever believe that I could help them? My feelings of insecurity, imposture syndrome, low self-efficacy, and confusion evolved, however, and became required fuel for my altered thoughts, desires, and subsequent actions at some unknown pit-stop in my journey.

There was one caveat, however: I only wanted to help people who had been hurt or challenged in a "different" way than me. As a result of this, I ended up aiding individuals with military combat-related trauma and/or psychotic spectrum disorder. Slowly but surely, I found myself guiding our nation's heroes through the process of recovery and re-entry into the civilian workforce as industry leaders. I was making a difference—me! This sort-of-broken clinician was making a difference, and it was such an amazing feeling. Was this how it felt when you landed on your purpose?

Notably, I was slowly but surely coming into contact with more and more people who had been physically abused and/or sexually assaulted. Military sexual trauma (MST) was, and continues to be, a tragedy, and I was at the front and center of the aftermath. Men and women who had put their lives on the line for our country would join me weekly in my purposefully amber-lit office as I welcomed them into the sacred and safe space where they could take off their superman and superwoman capes. They didn't always have the energy or mind to adjust their Clark Kent-style glasses before tears caught them off-guard. In these moments, I was witnessing the unfolding of my purpose. Like me, they thought they were broken—damaged, even. But I saw differently: like me, they had so much to offer the world—and like them, I discovered how much it meant to rise from the darkness, more powerful than one would have ever known possible. We all needed someone to truly see our needs, help us find our purpose, and step into our superpowers without guilt, confusion, or anything less than razor-sharp focus on impacting change in the lives of those we encounter.

So, there you have it. I decided to not only advocate for peace, but to help others move beyond their past towards the fulfillment of their purpose.

Confession: Every now and then, when I share pieces of my life, I actually wish I had a warm and fuzzy storyline about the moments I discovered the pieces of my purpose. In reality, coming to the realization that it was time for me to step into my superpower didn't feel any better than when I was in the midst of life struggles; after all, it takes grit, stone-cold determination, and sometimes blind-faith to follow your purpose, truly achieve a sustainable impact, and take care of yourself, all at the same time. I admittedly thought of killing myself several times during this process; it got pretty dark along the road of an almost-constant state of hopelessness. Regardless, I never attempted because I ultimately knew that this was all a part of the grand scheme of having a purpose, making sense of the physical, mental, and emotional pain, and building my resilience after being told *ad nauseum* that I wasn't going to live a fulfilling or functional life—*if* I so happened to survive childhood. I had to constantly encourage myself; pull it together; be strong; and yet there were times when I couldn't see any reason behind why I should do so. I truly had no internal drive to live this life that was so full of pain.

I remember the numbness that came with each external accomplishment; the confusion on the faces of family and friends when they could see I wasn't excited about graduating high school, undergrad, or graduate school, nor my doctoral program. They didn't understand the loneliness I felt during these times. I was stuck in an inescapable cycle of survival mode; I didn't know how to relax without triggering a panic attack. The insecurities that had been built up as a result of people sending messages, directly and indirectly, pertaining to my not being good enough, would always jar me out of any task or period in time that wasn't "productive" or "work".

While essentially suffering in silence, I was left with internal conflict, spiritual warfare, and, eventually, a miracle baby who required me to figure it out or choose generational damage—by *my* hands, this time.

Despite the many shiny objects I have attained—my doctorate; a home in LA; marriage; a career; a beautiful and healthy son—life was not what it appeared to be. Despite the "proof" that I was okay, finding my purpose led me to the deep, dark crevasses of a never-before-explored ocean floor. Suddenly, I was faced with a choice: either I had to begin feeling my way out through prayer and earnest spiritual grounding, or die trying.

At one point, it seemed pretty close to the latter: my marriage was ending, I was unable to fulfil my essential duties at work, I was traumatized by domestic violence, I was displaced out of my home during a pandemic, I was losing faith, and I had no clue that I'd soon be dealing with the death of my father—at the hand of COVID, no less.

It was while in this dark crevasse of despair that I truly began documenting what later became the backbone of my brand, signature programs, and overall approach for my business. In-between making sure that I ate, bathed, and attended intensive outpatient therapy, I either did one of two types of things: went for a run/walk around the neighborhood, or curated workbooks, self-care and mindfulness journals, self-assessments, guides, podcast recordings, ninety-day workbooks, and a few short worksheets that would prompt future clients to remove all excuses throughout their healing journey. My mom, who was helping to care for me and my son at the time, showed grace, amazement, and understanding for my need to feel "productive". I'd come out of my childhood bedroom showing off what I had accomplished while hidden away for hours, so, on a level of compassion and grace, this behavior must have made sense to her.

While mentally and emotionally processing the domestic violence I had endured (yielding my newfound diagnosis of PTSD), I realized that it wasn't until I prepared for healing that my chance at recovery would come to life. I envisioned what it might look like to return from this dark and isolated place; to find a new normal for my life as a newly single mom, healer, friend, sister, daughter, believer, spiritual vessel, and seeker of peace. It was going to be *different*. I couldn't settle for the intense wonder I felt towards all those who had a purpose-driven life; those who also had endured a series of what seemed like unfortunate events that merely produced a healing resolve. Therefore, I commenced developing my company mission that was one hundred percent catered to real people, real problems, and real transformation. My clients will find their way back to themselves and use faith to aim for purpose and gain clarity in their storm.

Deemed a leader in the fields of mental health and organizational development psychology, I spent some time leading up to the extended leave of absence, mining for and developing servant leaders while cultivating organizational health culture within the federal healthcare sector. For anyone wanting to use their tragedy as fuel for their purpose, I was ready and on fire! I knew it was time for my business to rise up, start igniting the healing process, and help purpose-driven leaders to step into their superpower and lead with intention.

While there is a science to it all, my clients start their journey by being led through a major mental and emotional detox: from daily brain-dumping, cognitive processing, and intensive coaching sessions, I use a combination of evidence-based techniques to help them safely push beyond their comfort zones and into the face of the various barriers thwarting their higher quality of life. While I have a separate Mental Detox Five-Day Challenge, slow and steady is certainly the way to go for those who have a lot to work through and need a coach along for the ride.

Notably, effective coping skills and support systems must be present, identifiable, and tested for effectiveness before going any deeper. Once these internal drivers are in place, we hit the road!

It won't take much time to realize that it's life's distractions and a pervasive state of survival that blocks creativity, transformation, and vision-fulfilment. Indeed, once this weight has been lifted, raising one's threshold of both personal and professional success will be just around the corner—and this time, it won't need to be done alone. With professional and personal experiences, being coached into greatness will take on a whole new meaning.

Now, should quick wins be expected during a slow and steady model? Absolutely. Every leader who is completing or has completed my programs have confirmed progress within a matter of seven to fourteen days of doing exactly as instructed. What must be understood here is that no matter the challenge, clarity of mind can lead to extraordinary levels of creativity, problem-solving, memory recall, and executive decision-making—all of which having the potential to be a sweet deal when you're operating in your gifts, talents, and purpose. My mission and role in the matter is to help reduce feelings of overwhelm and hopelessness amongst top influencers who quite simply need to find their way out of the darkness to reset and have their hidden visions, passions, and purpose come to life.

I now must give a disclaimer and state that I understand that all of this sounds unreal and too good to be true—but that's the best part! I consider myself to be a realist who has also come to understand the balance and treasures found at the intersection of faith and wisdom. While there are many stories of triumph out there, I have found none of them, especially not my own, have come easy; rather, the power lies in simply *not giving up* when it seems unbearable. During my own low points, I felt, and even sometimes believed, that my existence on this earth had not been for my passions alone. However, when you've reached rock-bottom (as I believe I have on multiple occasions), questions of *why am I still here?* do end up getting answered. As for me, I have maintained much-needed anchoring within my faith; in this way, I've grown wiser and more willing to see the intangible forces and influence of God, who has drawn every last one of my clients to me in a truly miraculous way.

As I witness my clients becoming bold and achieving a true sense of work–life balance and harmonious state of living, they've all shared their own stories of doors opening for them in very extraordinary ways—sometimes all in sync—which I will forever attribute to divine alignment. Indeed, I have a very humbling and unique purpose that helps me to wake up each morning and try again. Instead of chronic suicidal ideation, dissonance, and hopelessness, I get to wake up to my miracle baby and help servant leaders across the world lighten the load that may have been slowly dragging them into burnout, so that instead, they can grab hold of their purpose and vision. This has allowed me to leave my nine-to-five, as well as to safeguard myself from being triggered or discriminated against: I work only with those who are sent to me for holistic support, which, by divine assignment means that I can fulfill my purpose on an international level, curate each day as my own boss, and coach my ideal clients along their transformation journey.

Oftentimes, when being interviewed or contacted about my service offerings, I still find myself thanking each and every prospective client for considering me for their coaching and consultative needs. It's still humbling, really! While I understand and am fully aware of how long I was in school (twelve years post-high school) and how much of an investment it was to study, practice, and become certified in all my areas of expertise (this process taking an additional seven years), I can't ever take credit from the brave and strong folks who have actually trusted me to help them on such a private and life-changing chapter in their lives. Some even decide to stay with me for even longer for maintenance work along the way, given their desire to establish their newfound lifestyle habits while also gambling with the possibility of when it remains good practice to check in. Either way, it's a pretty unique road that must be traveled, and I give space for every client's individualized needs in return.

I must say that I'm much like a unicorn in my lane, considering I've been through so much in my life, all while managing a chronic medical condition and near-death experiences while still achieving professional milestones. But I prefer not to advertise the shiny objects or fluffy, feel-good stuff. Instead, I want to extend my disclaimers and notice to people who may read this story and consider working with me. My focus is on *real* transformation as a conduit to *real* growth, success, and life purpose-fulfilment. My fellow female executives must be ready to dig deep, do the work, and stay for the entire course until new habits have been formed.

The latter stage is where people usually fall off for one reason or another.

With that said, I do not allow those contracted with me to fall off the wagon before they ever leave the station—and that is what often happens when the power of change and transformation is not effectively implemented in typical coaching and consulting arrangements. I am legally and ethically bound to ensure (so long as you are my client and engaged in my services) that you take part in evidence-based practices designed to move you from the basics to the full-blown lifestyle you've always envisioned.

Taking it a step further, for those who are ready, I'm a master's-level advanced practice licensed clinical social work therapist (you see why I just say psychotherapist— too many words!), and I've spent the first leg of my professional career studying and treating the dynamic conditions that fall within the latest revision of the

Diagnostic and Statistical Manual (DSM). I have been certified in marriage and family therapy (MFT) techniques, military sexual trauma (MST) therapy techniques, and practical applications for intimate relationship (PAIRS) skills, and am internationally certified as an alcohol and drug counselor (ICADC) and in conflict resolution, clinical and administrative debriefing techniques, mentoring, and master-level transformational coaching—all of this being prior to my obtaining a doctorate in organizational development psychology with a specialization in executive coaching and leadership.

So, when I tell you that I understand the human capacity and specific environment in which sustainable change may occur in a work setting, I mean business!

I have made a point of cultivating all of my knowledge, skills, expertise, and life experiences into the services and products I have created to empower and equip female executives with everything they need. All that's required of my clients is for them to be ready to do the work; to come to the table with a hunger for *more*. Life is not going to get any easier or suddenly fall into alignment because that's all you've been praying for *ad nauseum*. Just as I had to step away, really dump the waste that was in my head, and pick up all the things that contribute to my purpose, female executives who are ready to reclaim the time wasted on diluted and shiny offers for quick success are those who will benefit from connecting with me and getting a copy of my carefully crafted Work-Life Balance Accelerator, a ninety-day workbook and daily planner.

In an effort to jumpstart motivation and alignment with the type of investment necessary for this level of work, getting started with this free product will push you closer to mental, emotional, and spiritual alignment— slow and steady, but giving you the low-hanging fruit needed to keep you engaged and ready to go deeper and further into the light. It *is* time to step out of that dark place that drew you here in the first place. When you're ready, you'll have everything you need to make that call and get started with your first one-on-one with me. So, get ready to face your fears, get curious regarding your purpose, and do the work needed to reignite the spirit of high moral and ethical leading that yields impact, transformation, and vision-fulfilment in your life as well as those waiting to raise their quality of life because of your gift(s).

Contact Shané

www.officialspcg.com

facebook.com/thespcgroup

facebook.com/groups/pursuitofpeacemovement

www.linkedin.com/in/thespcgroup

www.twitter.com/thespcgroup_

www.instagram.com/thespcgroup

drshanepetite@gmail.com

Shané's Resources

Work-Life Balance Accelerator: A 90-Day Guide and Planner for Leaders Driving Sustainable Change: bit.ly/envisionpeace

MARIE KUENY

Founder & CEO of Compassionate Educators and Licensed School Counselor

"Three little pigs, three little pigs, let me in!"

I was five years old, and the nightmares wouldn't cease: the big bad wolf in my dreams wasn't a mythical talking creature, but none other than my own father.

The dreams included images of him locking my mom in her own purse, from which I couldn't help her. In other nightmares, I was falling into nothingness, everything empty as a black hole around me, and all I could hear was his laughter echoing in the background. Not quite the fairy tale life that little girls without a father picture their lives to be if their dad was around! Instead, I wished and hoped that I was adopted, or that I could run away to escape the clamp squeezing my heart and soul. Hearing the cries of my mom and little brother during one of his raging episodes was more than my gentle nature could take—so at the ripe age of nine, I packed up my backpack, ready to make a run for it.

My father wasn't pure evil: I truly believe that he tried to love us, but his own significant trauma and mental illness got in the way on almost a daily basis. Regardless, hearing him scream at my mom, her cries, his rage, her depression, his abuse, her bruises, his rollercoaster ride of emotions that we all were trapped in, meant I wanted out. I *needed* out. Desperately.

As a child, I loved reading. Okay, I was *obsessed* with reading. Books were a way for me to break free from the life I didn't want to be in and to be transported anywhere but there.

So, there I was at nine years old, reading *From the Mixed-Up Files of Mrs. Basil E. Frankweiler*, about a twelve-year-old girl and her nine-year-old brother who ran away to the Metropolitan Museum of Arts. I felt hope welling up in my heart—this nervous, excited feeling that maybe I, too, could be like the Kincaids and find a new safe place to escape to. My adventurous spirit was set ablaze!

Every day, I worked on hatching my plans to run away to a new life. First, I would need supplies, such as food that would not need refrigeration—so I grabbed an old backpack and started to hoard items in it slowly so that my mom wouldn't notice: a bag of donuts; my favorite Barbie doll; a juice box; a book or two (of course!). I was a pretty independent nine-year-old, but I was still only nine. I didn't quite have the background of a survivalist.

So, there I was, secretly devising my strategy. I would leave after dinner, but not before it got too dark outside. My journey would start with my running to the Piggly Wiggly grocery store a few blocks away. I would then hide out there during closing time; that way, I had a safe, warm place to stay and didn't have to rely only on my bag of donuts for my only nourishment. The snack aisles would be all mine! I would then find a new community and start working to earn money and...

I truly can't recall what came next in my plan, but I knew that I had to get into a stable situation first. Then, I would somehow send for my little brother and we would live happily ever after, without my barbaric dad ruining our lives. I knew I would miss my mom, but all I could focus on was keeping my brother and I safe from the abuse and misery.

The day finally came when I felt the courage to go for it. I was going to wait on the back porch until the right time, backpack in hand, and then scale the two-story wall down and charge for the grocery store.

Great plan, right?

I was outside on the porch trying to hide behind the patio chair for maybe five minutes when my mom found me.

"What are you doing, Marie?"

Well, *that* didn't work.

I started sobbing. I told her that I couldn't live like this anymore; I couldn't bear to see him hurt her anymore. I couldn't sit there while he hit my brother and called me awful names. I needed to get out; I needed to run away from it all.

She listened quietly as I told her my plans of leaving. It came down to me giving the ultimatum, "It's either me or him."

She chose me.

In truth, she chose herself and her children; she chose to take her *power* back.

My mom was a victim, but she was also a powerhouse woman that got lost in a toxic relationship when she attempted to fill an empty hole in her own heart.

My mom had attempted to leave her abuser—my father—so many times, but it wasn't until that night that she would leave him once and for all and never turn back.

It was also from that moment that I recognized the power I had within myself—the power to make a difference; the power to shine a light on the dark spaces that needed to be aired out; the power to make transformational change, even as a young child.

As I moved into my teen years and adulthood, I encountered more traumatic experiences, from sexual assault at sixteen to unwittingly stepping into a toxic relationship in my late twenties—but each and every time that I found myself in the center of darkness—sometimes so dark that I contemplated, even fantasized at times, of ending this life—I could see the light, even if it was just a memory of a glimmer of light shining in the distance.

When my mom stepped out onto that porch, I finally no longer felt alone; I realized that the power we had collectively could get us through anything. I also realized that nothing ever stays the same, which means that as excruciating as those moments felt—as heartbreaking as some of my experiences had been—the pain would not— *could* not, by the laws of the universe—last forever.

By the time I was a teenager, I knew that my mission in this life was to help others to see their own light and to be a vehicle of positive change and hope, especially for women and children. I clearly saw myself as a catalyst for change that could make an impact that would outlast my time on Earth.

After a while, my nightmares and flashbacks of the trauma began to wane and were replaced with beautiful, bold dreams of the life I wanted to create for myself—one where I inspired other women to leave their abusers and helped children to open their eyes and hearts to what was possible for them; one where I created movements that would foster healing and renewal—not to mention one where I traveled around the globe, connecting with other heart-centered folks that wanted to create more joy, freedom, and healing in this world.

I could envision myself being in a loving relationship with a partner who encouraged me, using their words and touch for love and connection. I saw children in my life laughing and playing, able to leave adult worries to the adults while they safely explored their environments to discover what made their hearts happy and full.

Knowing that I didn't have to continue the generational cycles of abuse and that it could end with me provided me with so much strength throughout my journey: life didn't have to happen *to* me without my consent; without my acceptance. Indeed, the more I allowed my dreams and hopes to expand, the more I became a creator of my own destiny. The more I focused on what I *did* want—happiness, security, adventure, courage, and love—opportunities and people were presented to me that have allowed me to create a life of my choosing.

Knowing from a young age that my mission was to serve and support others, during my junior year of high school, I became a "volunteer" at a local runaway shelter—a true full-circle moment.

When it was time for me to choose a college major, I knew that I wanted to serve children—so elementary education was where I began. I then changed to a social work major, however, as I learned about the firsthand support I could provide for families who were in crisis.

After several years of direct services with families, from providing in-home parenting and community resources to taking teen moms to their doctor appointments and helping women to gain independence from abusive partners, I went back to university: my heart was still pulling in the direction of work in the school system: teachers, after all, had been heroes to me in childhood, showcasing a life that was full of compassion and kindness—not to mention travel and intellectual pursuits. Teachers had always been my role models and the type of people I wanted to be surrounded by every day. I also knew that school was the place that children spent the majority of their time aside from home and, in some cases, even more than home, so I saw incredible potential in the school system to make a significant difference.

Taking the best of both worlds as a social worker and an educator, I obtained my master's degree in educational psychology and became licensed as a school counselor. Several months after graduating, I accepted a job offer as a freshmen intervention counselor.

I loved it. Although I was split between two high schools that had more needs than I could possibly cover, I poured my heart into the students I worked with, doing everything in my power to make their transitions as smooth as possible. I dedicated those years to helping them to find the motivation to pursue their own goals and dreams despite the traumas and hardships they had encountered.

As I mentioned before, though, change is inevitable, and my dream job, as I truly felt it was at the time, came to an end: the politics in my state changed and became incredibly heated, and my position, along with over two hundred more in my district, vanished overnight. On top of my job loss, I became swept into a relationship that fueled depression, anxiety, and loneliness, leaving an empty shell of who I had worked so hard to become. Add to that the shame and embarrassment I felt when I realized I was *in* an unhealthy relationship, and I was left with the question of how I could possibly help others when I couldn't even help myself at that moment in time. I had lost my job, I was losing friends who didn't want to hear about my relationship struggles anymore, and I was losing self-confidence and self-respect. The darkness was surrounding me as I again found myself in a place of despair.

Then, the light appeared—well, a memory of the light, rather, as I was close to losing hope that my life would ever be better. Sometimes, our minds can play those kinds of trick on us.

I knew I needed help: I couldn't attempt to pick myself up anymore; I needed to create a support team, just as I had taught the women who I had worked with to do.

Hence, utilizing a local women's resource center, a good friend, a cousin, and, no doubt, my mom, to hold me up and keep myself accountable for making the changes I needed in my life, I was saved from going further down the path of despair. Mix in a little survivor music from Christina Aguilera and Rachel Platten with a few online mindset courses and some meditation practice, and I found I could finally breathe again—but this time, as a single mom.

Now that I was released from the clutches of a man

who wanted to own me, I could focus on my health, my healing, and get back to pursuing my dreams, once again putting the nightmares to rest. My local school district opened their hiring doors again and I accepted a position at a dual-language elementary school. My heart was full!

Unlike my first counseling position, where I was one hundred percent focused on the students' needs, I began to see a sector of school that I had had blinders on previously. The teachers and staff were exhausted, giving every ounce of time and energy to their students while struggling to care for their own physical wellbeing and mental health. I recall one year when I went to see a therapist to work on healing my traumas, I saw two more co-workers in the waiting room of the mental health office. As a naturally curious person, I began asking myself, *Why?* Why is the therapist's waiting room filled with school staff?

As I dug deeper into examining both my personal experiences as well as academic research, the connection became clear: many school staff members experienced burnout, compassion fatigue, and secondary trauma while on the job, but it was rarely ever discussed. Indeed, when we don't have awareness about what lies beneath the surface, it's almost impossible to heal. Shedding light on the struggles may be painful at first, but it's the only way to heal and is a lot less painful than living a life of suffering.

Another realization occurred to me at this time: teaching is a very isolating profession. Sure, teachers flock together and often bond outside of school, but the role itself can be very lonely: teachers are often in a room for hours every day without any other adult interaction. Meanwhile, when it comes to support roles, such as school counselors, school social workers, and school psychologists, these people are often the only ones in the building in that role, which leads to another complex type of isolation which one special education teacher described as feeling like "a lonely island". I know that administrators share a similar experience, as they are expected to have all the answers to questions and concerns that no one prepared them for. So who do they go to when they are in need?

No one wants to admit that they need help. As adults, we are supposed to have it all together, right? Well, this simply is a facade. After working with countless educators across the globe, I have concluded that no one has all of the answers and that everyone has moments (or even years) when they want to throw their hands up and be done. In fact, most sources claim that between thirty percent and fifty percent of teachers leave the profession within the first five years of being in the profession. I ask again, why?

There are many reasons for this that we can discuss another day, but let's instead explore how we can shift the dynamics for our superheroes in crisis. I was once taught by a Zen Buddhist teacher to always ask the question, "How can I help?" It was through this question that Compassionate Educators was developed: I desired to create a community where educators everywhere could share openly in a safe and supportive environment. I also wanted to share with teachers the incredible insights and discoveries I had made as a school counselor, social worker, and trauma thriver so that they could apply the most effective strategies to their own classrooms. I envisioned a space where we could celebrate wins, overcome challenges, and brainstorm ways that we and our students could thrive all year long, regardless of external circumstances.

In fact, many teachers who leave the classroom return to the profession in some shape or form—but what if you could gain the confidence, skills, and work-life balance without needing to take a sabbatical to "find yourself" first? What if you already had everything you need; it's just a matter of building the support system around you and learning how to stop the time and energy drain that impacts so many in this field?

When teachers and staff first enter The Compassionate Educators Leadership Program, they are usually exhausted by the demands in their careers, struggling to find time for sleep, nourishment, and friends and family, and often are questioning their own skills in leadership, student behavior management, and/or their ability to hold space and boundaries as their career engulfs every aspect of their lives. They also all have one key element in common: a fire deep within to serve their students and be the best teacher they can be, even if that fire has just become a smolder of an ember after years of feeling underappreciated and overworked.

Within the program, which is typically between six and twelve months, teachers are given the tools to assess their support systems and energy levels and reconnect to their purpose, which, strategically combined, has the opportunity to expand their time, energy, and joy. Together, we dive deep into examining the impacts that trauma can have on ourselves and our students, as well as ways of practicing compassion for others and ourselves. Topics such as emotional regulation in the classroom, inclusion and community-building, and elevating confidence and assertiveness skills, are infused into our time together.

One of the most beautiful aspects of The Compassionate Educators Leadership Program isn't even what I give, but is the space that is held for the community to give and receive from one another. There is a sense of unity in knowing that others around the country are going through similar experiences, which is quite cathartic in its own right.

Members of the program meet weekly on a virtual platform to learn from myself and one another, to celebrate their successes in student achievement and their personal and professional wins, and to be there for one another when times are tough. This is exactly the kind of community I wish I had years ago and is precisely why I deliberately designed the program to be an amazing source of not only professional development but of personal expansion, too.

The results that teachers gain as a result of The Compassionate Educators Program have been phenomenal: upon reflecting on their participation, educators have said, "After implementing the strategies that were suggested by Marie... I am able to get everything I need done in less time and being less exhausted," and, "Having the team-building experience with the Compassionate Educator teachers from around the world... That's just such a benefit. You realize that no matter where you are, where you teach, or how long you've been teaching, we all have such similar situations in some ways. It's so nice to realize you are in it together."

I truly believe that everything happens for a reason. During those years as a child, my enduring challenges that I wanted to run away from led me to not only see the power I have within, but also to understand the struggles that others experience; they have helped me to learn how to lead others through challenges and see the interconnectedness of all of our stories, dreams, and sorrows. Throughout it all is always light—even if this is just a memory of light.

After five years of no contact with my biological father and much work healing my own emotional wounds, I took a deep breath and called him. He told me to protect my children in the same way that my mother protected me. He wished us safety and expressed regret that he hadn't been a better father.

The circle is complete: I can fully move on with my whole heart intact.

The future I am planning is one in which educators acknowledge their own power, shine their lights, and collectively create more opportunities for children to be seen, heard, and valued so that they never even question the powerful, positive impacts that they can make on Earth and humankind.

For my Compassionate Educators community, I will continue to serve as a facilitator and guide, with the intention of expanding services each year until every educator feels seen, heard, and valued. I will also continue to host my podcast, *The Compassionate*

Educators Show, which provides additional skills, tools, and mindset shifts with guest experts. Several exciting additions that will soon be unveiled include releasing *The Compassionate Educators Guide,* dedicated to expanding on the strategies I have found to be fundamental in creating a thriving school environment for both staff and students. Additionally, be on the lookout for an enriching, luxurious retreat that will be available in the summer to Compassionate Educators! During these retreats, teachers will be pampered and invited to refill their energy buckets while connecting with other amazing educators who understand the need to release the stress of the school year.

I have received so many blessings and opportunities along my journey that the traumas I've encountered give me even more reason to shower those I am connected to with as much compassion and support as I can.

If my story and mission resonate with you, I invite you to check out a special gift I have curated for you. When you go to www.compassionateeducators.com/gift, you will have the opportunity to download a free energy assessment, which will help you to uncover where your energy blocks and leaks are so that you can protect your most precious asset during the school year and discover how to create your ideal work-life balance.

One more thing before we say goodbye for now: if you want a glimpse into The Compassionate Educators community, check out our free group at www.compassionateeducators.com/group, where you can learn more about applying the principles of compassionate education so that you and your students thrive.

Contact Marie

www.compassionateeducators.com

www.facebook.com/MarieCrystalKueny

www.facebook.com/groups/
compassionateeducationresources

www.linkedin.com/in/marie-kueny-b1a4b993

@Marie_Kueny

@CompassionateEducators

support@compassionateeducators.com

Marie's Resources

The Compassionate Educators' Energy Assessment:
www.compassionateeducators.com/gift

SASHA SERENE

Mindshift Healer and Entrepreneur

I REMEMBER FEELING LIKE an oddball growing up; as though I never belonged anywhere. It was because of this that I was always quiet.

Little did I know that, by the age of six, I had learned to suppress my emotions, never really speaking to anyone unless spoken to, almost living expressionless due to my fear of being judged or dismissed. I was bullied—often called the weirdo; loner; different—and frequently guilt-tripped into doing (or not doing) something simply because it would be beneficial for the other person.

It was after many years of such events that I began to

wonder what was wrong with me: Why was I so angry? Why did I cry so much? Was I broken? Self-harm became my escape, and yet I always kept these actions and struggles to myself: I didn't want anyone thinking I was crazy.

To top everything off, I acted as somewhat of an emotional parent for my mom from childhood and throughout my teenage years—something that was extremely difficult and meant I had to constantly upkeep an appearance of everything being okay, even if "okay" couldn't have been further from the truth. *Be happy. Stop crying. What are you, stupid?*

I couldn't have my own voice due to my immense responsibility and embarrassment.

Between the ages of twelve and thirteen, my mother remarried. This was a surprise but also somewhat of a relief: I didn't want her to be alone. However, I quickly found myself to be fourteen and thinking, *Why is he in my bedroom the morning of my birthday? Is he really commenting on me becoming a woman? This is uncomfortable; the energy of this is all off! Why is he hugging me? Why is he rubbing my back under my shirt?*

By the time nineteen came around, I'd had several partners, always with the aim of feeling loved, wanted, accepted, and cared for. One such relationship led to my agreeing to marry him—and just a month before, I couldn't help but wonder how nobody was stopping this; how *I* wasn't stopping this. After all, he'd certainly shown his violent tendencies.

Regardless of these doubts, I saw no other option but to proceed with the ceremony: the AirForce was out of the question (I had previously asked my mom and received the guilt-inducing response, "Who's going to help me now?"), my mom felt universities were too dangerous, and community colleges were too far away. I didn't have a car and barely knew how to drive, let alone get around the city.

These options considered and subsequently dismissed, I concluded, *Sure, I'll get married. If anything, it'll be a challenge.*

During the first year of our marriage, there were moments when I couldn't explain why my husband was so angry; why my hands got clammy when I spoke with him; why I had anxiety that would build up in my chest. I was responsible for keeping him out of trouble, like the time when we became homeless because he'd decided to act tough, leading us to be removed from corporate housing. I came to realize that, most of the time, he spoke *at* me, not *with* me. He used to say that he loved to see me cry since I looked so pretty when I did.

Looking back, there was a sense of resentment that formed the foundation of our relationship.

The violence never stopped. I fought back—but mentally and emotionally, I was a wreck, and I didn't know how to feel anything but numb half the time.

Perhaps predictably, my occasional fighting back always made things worse, and our alcohol consumption didn't help, since this amplified everything for both of us. Hurt people hurt people, after all. I never felt I could say *no* to him due to my fear of being ridiculed, judged, bullied, or picked on by him, so I went along with everything he wanted, letting myself go numb; acting; pretending; hiding my emotions.

I distinctly remember the day I realized I wanted out—for sure this time. We were driving down the main street and, of course, we were intoxicated—him more than me—when we got into an argument. By this point, I knew not to react to him—it would only make things worse—but, for some reason, he wouldn't stop swinging for me, keeping one hand on the steering wheel.

For a moment, everything stopped: there was no yelling; no music; no noise. It was almost like everything was in slow motion. I found myself taking off my seatbelt, unlocking and opening the passenger door, and watching the white lines of the lane go by. I wanted out.

I felt numb to what was happening. Why was I even alive? What was the point? There was nothing out there for me. Why was I still here? This would never stop; he would never change; I would never be able to leave.

My childhood hadn't been as physically abusive as this, but it had felt just like this moment: numb. After all, on paper, I was doing all the same things: dressing up to be accepted by society; acting how I thought people expected me to; struggling with how to express my emotions—only this time, I did so through drinking, mindless sex, serving in my place of work, making sure everyone else was okay, and constantly trying to attain the approval of those who didn't like me.

As this was all playing in my head, somehow, he yanked me back into the car by my hair, hitting me like a ton of bricks (literally and metaphorically) as I realized one of us was certainly going to end up either dead or in jail.

I crawled into the back seat of the car, where I considered to be the furthest corner from him and thus where he couldn't reach me. He drove us to the house and I refused to go in, sleeping in the car.

Week in and week out, there was always some form of abuse: violence; drama; suppression; black eyes; bumps and bruises; bite marks; scratches; fingerprints from where he had gripped me too tightly. I remember during a particularly bad weekend, he woke up in the morning, turned to me, and immediately went to the store to purchase concealer for my face, stating he couldn't remember anything from the night before.

I couldn't even look at myself. I was broken.

Later that week, I went to my corporate job looking perfectly fine and well-put-together, a smile painted on my face. I'd become somewhat of a makeup professional through the online videos I watched. To outsiders looking in, nothing was wrong; I was perfectly intact— that is, until I went to the bathroom to touch up spots here and there and the reality of my life came crashing back down around me.

I couldn't see myself living like this anymore; it had been eight years, and this wasn't how my life was supposed to be lived. I didn't deserve this: I deserved to be free, not caged. I deserved more than what he thought of me... but then again, what did I even think of myself?

During this period, my mom moved in with us—and it was at this moment that it truly felt like everything was falling apart: no one was getting along, and there was tension in every corner of the house. I knew my mom needed to get out of there. *I* needed to get out of there.

My mom only ever caught a glimpse of him yelling at me. "Is this how you want to keep living?" she asked. *Oh, Mom, you have no idea.*

It was a few months later that I told her the full extent of the abuse, and it was after this that we found a storage unit and moved the majority of my things into it, simultaneously searching for a place for the both of us to sleep that week—all while still going to work, with no one knowing what was happening.

We ended up at a hotel, where we stayed for a few weeks: I couldn't find a place to rent and my head wasn't in the right place; my insecurities were oozing out of me like never before. This was the second time I had been homeless—and yet, to this day, I am still so grateful I was able to get a room to share with my mom, with her on one side and me on the other. Somehow, we made it work by staying out of each other's way.

It took me three months to find a house.

When I went back to my husband's house to collect the rest of my stuff, nothing had changed: he was hurt; I was hurt. He had anger; I had anger. He needed to heal; I needed to heal.

That was the last time he laid his hands on me, and even throughout the act, I remained strong over my decision. Even as I was trapped between a wooden door while trying to get out of the house, I didn't react—and that following Monday, with a bruise on my upper arm, I showed up to work, ready for the next chapter—this time living with my mom ten years after leaving home at nineteen.

This presented a whole new level of healing,

boundaries, mindset shifts, inner work, and self-discovery. I realized I needed to stop being a people-pleaser and drinking and that I needed to take responsibility for my life. This proved to be very hard: I would keep drinking and then quit drinking, and I'd blame my mom for being this way and that way. I'd go to clubs, sometimes alone, since it was my form of escapism. Traumas from childhood remained unhealed.

However, I saw more for myself than this.

I started to make changes.

For two years, I rented an apartment smack in the middle of downtown Kansas City. I was still doing tons of inner work on my own, and most importantly, I started to share my story; somehow, I knew that sharing my story with others would help them to see where I was coming from. Opening up can lead to someone gaining perspective over their own experience—perspective that things can change. I knew I also wanted to leave the corporate world and instead help change the lives of people that felt unsupported or emotionally overwhelmed, invest in real estate, and somehow become a global entrepreneur. Hence, on top of helping people who were struggling internally, I tapped into a real estate investment education company that, to me, is like no other. I incorporated and leveraged their self-development into my life, and through them I met one of

Kansas City's most highly rated life coaches, with whom I began to peel back the layers that felt like a thousand pounds, healing as I had never done before in my life.

After six months of phone calls (the majority of which I spent crying), the last day of my coaching with him arrived. My heart dropped: who was going to hold space for me now? I've held space for many people close to me, but I still felt I needed someone—until I realized *I could hold space for myself*; it just starts with being my own best friend!

"Have you ever thought of becoming a life coach?" my coach asked on our last call. "You have a gift for holding space for those who are hurting."

I actually laughed down the phone at this idea. Me, doing this for others? As a service? Nah.

One year after that conversation, I was still connected to the real estate investment education group, simultaneously completing the inner work my coach had taught me, listening to podcasts, and reading self-help books—when, one day, I came across an empowerment event my coach had coming up. I attended.

All of a sudden, the universe aligned me with a vision I had had not too long ago: I wanted to help others to amplify their true selves in this world of ours. He asked for anyone who was thinking of becoming a coach to reach out to him.

So, what did I do? I took the leap of faith: I certified myself as a coach under his practice. There was even more healing to do than that which I had already embarked on, but I kept going, and slowly but surely, my beliefs started changing and my mind shifted even more: my compassion for people magnified by ten times, and I began to recognize that *everyone is on their own journey.* In light of this realization, I found I wanted to work with people from all different backgrounds. When I look at someone, I see that, behind every person lies a story of ambitions, fears, goals, and setbacks. To me, everyone's journey is anything but ordinary.

My mind, body, and soul keep healing to this day. I chose to be safe; I chose to remain on our earth to share with you that it *is* possible to thrive beyond your wildest dreams. Through this journey and by putting one foot in front of the other, I've found my voice: no longer do I suppress my feelings; instead, I acknowledge them. The mindset that held me hostage back then I have now replaced with the mindset of choosing to design my own life. Now, I drink coffee almost every morning on my porch, meditating in my own time. Now, I feel safe in voicing what's happening within me internally without feeling a sense of hostility or insecurity: I've rewired my subconscious with conscious actions that have helped me to release the patterns from childhood that no longer serve me.

Seeing people who I've coached shift their perspective after one conversation and hearing them say, "I guess I never really looked at it that way. You've gotten further with me than anyone else because they just try to 'fix' me. Thank you for the work you do," is absolutely what keeps me going. Being the catalyst for others who previously thought they couldn't live what they saw in their minds or hearts is indescribable.

Through this foundational work, my goal is to help others to achieve a transformational shift by providing mental and emotional support via a safe space for entrepreneurs who are overwhelmed, struggling, and want to grow themselves or their business (or both collectively). When I myself commenced on this healing journey, the doors started to open up in a way I never thought was possible: I became a theta healer, and through it, I helped the mind, body, and soul to clear away any limiting beliefs. With this spiritual philosophy, I replaced a belief of my own unworthiness with a belief that it is truly wonderful to be alive. Now, I know I am worthy.

Here is a mantra for you to speak when looking to embark on such a transformation:

I understand the definition of being heard by others
through the Creator of All That Is
I understand what it feels like to be heard by others
I know when to be heard by others
I know how to be heard by others
I know how to live my daily life heard by others
I know it is possible to be heard by others
I am heard by others
I have something worthwhile to say to others and
know it will be heard through the Creator of All That Is.

In a nutshell, my mission is to coach emotionally drained entrepreneurs to internally embody their most BeYouToFully Empowered selves so that they can grow and change the world around them. It's time to release the genetic programs that no longer serve you, this planet, or your children.

You know you're a badass; that you want to change the world around you; that you're committed; that you have been in Survival Mode... so let me ask you: when was the last time you struggled with being mentally or emotionally drained, or both?

Imagine turning that feeling into a gift or opportunity.

I truly and deeply believe, deep in my core, in the possibility of transformational mindset-shift on an emotional, spiritual, and mental level. I believe in breaking free from negative thought patterns, self-beliefs, and self-imposed limitations. I believe that *you* have the power to become a BeYouToFull leader in your industry—a leader that is self-confident, healed, and knows what she wants. I believe that by becoming a BeYouToFull leader, you can tangibly change the world around you, leave a legacy for future generations, and heal the cultural conditionings that have pervaded your previous generations. This process takes time—you will need to put in the work and effort to become the ripple, burn the chains, plant your seed, and work internally so that you can change your world externally—but I can say from experience that the process will be so incredibly worth it.

It is because of these beliefs that I engage in ninety-minute Expression Sessions with all of my prospective clients, just so we can establish whether we're a good fit for one another. If we are, we commit to each other for as long as it takes for them to become the most BeYouToFully empowered leaders they can be.

If this is a journey that you feel ready to commence—that is, if you're ready to become a BeYouToFully empowered leader—I would love to extend an invitation to you for one of such session.

To close, my journey has been one of challenges and the route to overcoming those challenges. It has been a test of resilience and strength, courage and inner-love, and it is one I ultimately believe I have passed with flying colors.

Life so far has taught me all about survival and the growth that waits for us in the wake of hardship. But it has also taught me about thriving and how embarking on that leg of the journey is a choice. Now thriving and helping others to thrive, I truly am where I am supposed to be.

Contact Sasha

 sashaserene.com

 www.facebook.com/sashaeserene

 sasha@sahaserene.com

CANDACE MAE

Leadership & Strategic Business Consultant, Executive Coach, and Speaker

I AM A RED-HEADED, feisty, outgoing woman who, from a very early age, felt unwanted, unloved, and unworthy. I was constantly told by my four siblings that I wasn't part of the family (apparently proven by my bright red hair) and that I didn't belong (I was "different", according to them), and yet, for as far back as I can remember, I have held an inner conviction that I was meant to be something more and to restore love in this world—a world which had thus far brought me much pain, rejection, and abuse.

Abuse... it's such a harsh word—a word I don't want

to claim—yet I suffered through a number of difficulties from a very young age; daily molestation at four years of age at the hands of a neighborhood teenager whose mother babysat me while my own mother worked, and even witnessing a six-foot burning cross surrounded by KKK members, garbed in white robes and hoods, at six years of age. My father would ask me—his young daughter—on each birthday, "How did anyone get so goddamn ugly in [age] years?!", and much of my childhood consisted of spankings with any object that was available to hand. My mother often pulled me by the hair and threw me across the kitchen floor.

To me, all of this was normal, along with all the other tragedies I emotionally buried inside me—something the body does to protect us. At some point, however, this gift of repression and suppression becomes a disservice to us when we decide we want to be whole; to be free from resentment, bitterness, and hate. After all, to do so, we must engage with and heal those painful memories.

In my childhood home, my father gave me criticism, hostility, and ridicule, while my siblings modeled jealousy—yet my mother, while she certainly had her own share of criticism and hostility to give, consciously tried to offset my father's and siblings' comments by teaching me tolerance, encouragement, praise, and approval. This formed a very polarizing environment, and ultimately taught me early in life that life isn't fair, so don't expect it to be.

I suppose I was simply running away from all of my childhood pain when I uprooted myself at nineteen, packing my clothes and stereo into my yellow two-door Vega and driving 2,500 miles across the United States, from Michigan to California, with no connections at my destination. To me, this was my opportunity to be free; to not be held back by the thoughts, judgments, and second-guessing of those around me.

In a hypercritical, cynical world full of violence and hate, I sought to stand for love, hope, and joy. I knew deep inside that I was a person of value who valued others and sought to give value to others at a time when they desperately needed hope. Indeed, I was on an adventure to become my best self.

Life, like a rollercoaster, is full of twists, turns, sudden drops, and gruelingly slow climbs. Looking back at all I've endured, it's clear God's Angel Armies were surrounding me, providing opportunities and protection.

Regardless, life was anything but easy: three days before turning twenty-one, I gave birth to my eldest daughter and was ridiculed by my grandmother, who told me that my life was now wasted and that I didn't deserve the blessing of a honeymoon or happily ever after. Indeed, I suppose it isn't a surprise that I've always struggled with receiving acceptance and feelings of not being good enough.

Nevertheless, I married my baby's father—only to leave him when my daughter was three weeks old due to his abusive nature. When she was two, we reconnected as a family—an arrangement that lasted less than one year due to his never coming home one day, abandoning our family.

He returned to me two years later, when our daughter was four, claiming to be a born-again Christian and insisting on seeing his daughter—and so, after a three-month reintroduction to his daughter over weekly phone calls, I allowed him to have an in-person visit while I went to work—only to have her disclose an assault that she had endured on his behalf the very next day.

This was a traumatic time that led me to an emotional breakdown, triggering all my childhood trauma that had been repressed in its wake.

During the successful prosecution, it materialized that he had done this horrific act once before, during the time when he with us when she was two. It truly is a mother's agonizing nightmare to figure out how such a thing happened: there was only one day when she was two years old that he was left alone with her, and even then it was only for one hour so I could walk to the local market. Looking back, this may have been the reason why he subsequently abandoned our family: for fear of his treacherous act being discovered.

Fast-forward thirty years and I have graduated with a bachelor's and a master's degree. I've owned three homes, and raised my three children – and am now enjoying three beautiful grandchildren. I love what I do now, which is transforming people and organizations, the effects of which are rippling into families, communities, and the world as a whole. This is my passion: to manifest the love of Christ in a physical, emotional, and spiritual way whereby others can embrace His Truth and find value within themselves and in others. I bring this Love into the workplace and in practical ways, helping others to discover their values and creating workplace cultures where people are valued and thrive in their strengths. I am excited to be a part of something bigger and to be contributing to the harmony present within the services and products needed in this world.

Living and leading with love is more than theory or Kumbaya: it's defining what respect looks like; how we talk to each other; our body language; our facial expressions; our intentions; our unconscious biases. Truth be known, my passion is to explore and share how we can create Heaven on Earth by manifesting Jesus

Christ through His Holy Spirit as it works in, with, and through us, restoring our relationship with God, unveiling the lies, and sharing the Truth. God is real and God is good, while Satan has brought us lies and robbed us of our true identity, power, and inheritance. Satan destroys and makes us the prisoners of our own minds through addiction, insecurity, and shame. Christ, however, has brought us an escape from this tragedy. We can be restored to our true identity in Christ, with full dominion and power.

I've taken multiple leaps of faith in my life, each of which being prompted by that internal conviction that *there is more to life than just surviving*. I'm a cup-half-full kind of girl, and I always kept my vision one step ahead: what's the next best step to grow myself? How can I better provide for my children? I rarely wallow in difficult circumstances; rather, I look ahead to where I *want* to be, and I keep striving. I have a personal relationship with Jesus Christ; His Holy Spirit dwells in me. I speak to Him regularly and ask for guidance. It wasn't always that way, but now it's so much more enjoyable having Christ within me.

As I reflect, my vision has constantly evolved as I matured:

- As a young child, I had visions of harmony, diverse friendships, and loving families.
- At eighteen, my vision was to become the best person I could be, express love for all people, and use my God-given gifts and talents, and create a home with a husband and children.
- In my twenties and as a single mom, I had visions of helping the homeless, teaching life skills, helping women and children to establish a steady home environment, and learning the skills necessary for building a career. I did a lot of work through the local church during this time, also volunteering at the Food Bank and teaching at Sunday School.
- In my thirties and forties, while married and then again as a single mom, my vision turned to obtaining my master's degree, building my career (to support my children in comfort). I wanted to make a difference and leave a legacy of change and hope for a brighter tomorrow for my children and the future generations to come – so I began preparing and envisioning my own business.
- Now, in my fifties, I own my own business, and I'm creating opportunities to travel the world, and am a philanthropic leader. My vision is to put my education, gifts, talents, resources, and experience into action so I can continue to transform my life and the lives of those around me. My vision is to equip leaders, business

owners, executives, and women in leadership to become their best selves, focusing on leaders and their teams to maximize my impact.

Indeed, developing leadership skills increases morale, productivity, and positive customer experiences; plus, the skills carry over into personal relationships, family, and the community, in turn positively impacting the world for multiple generations to come.

In light of my hardships, I have been working on personal growth since I was thirteen—and yet it was just last year, at fifty-eight, when I discovered some unconscious beliefs that were no longer serving me that limited what choices I saw as being available to me and held me back. It was these beliefs that kept manifesting events that would create self-fulfilling prophecies of sorts, confirming:

- I am alone.
- I have no one to help me.
- I cannot trust anyone. (This was the foundation of my anger and sadness.)
- I am rejected, unwanted, and unworthy.
- I am ashamed of sexual behavior (since I was forced to engage in it during my younger years and I engaged in it in my older years to receive acceptance, love, and worth).
- If I slow down my brain, I will develop learning

difficulties.
- I can't.
- I have no control; I must comply.
- Something must be wrong with me.
- I cannot get "free" help from others or they will think I am greedy.

When I left home at nineteen, I carried with me all these unconscious beliefs that I didn't even know were inside me. During this time, I was confrontational with others—a reactionary response I developed while verbally fighting my father when he would make bigoted remarks and prejudiced comments when I was younger. If you spoke with my adult children, they would tell you that I was abusive in my younger years: I spanked my kids; I raised my voice; I would confrontationally demand engagement and responses from partners who were gaslighting me. After an outburst of "righteous anger", I would be calm and happy, as if nothing happened, while those around me were still processing the tremors my outburst had caused. I didn't think I was abusive at the time: I looked at my intentions and knew I was just protecting myself. In other words, I gave myself the benefit of the doubt—yet when looking at others, I would solely focus on their observable behavior.

In my journey to becoming my best self, I discovered that growth is a lifelong process; there is no "end" as such. Rather, we must continue to grow until the day we die, for the day we stop growing is the day we start dying.

I love what I do, and with over twenty years of experience with leading cross-functional teams and managing system implementations, integrations, and reengineering processes, I've learned a wealth about managing change and influencing people. Most notably, I have learned that the importance of communication can't be stressed enough: communication is more than the transference of information; it's about connecting with others, being vulnerable, and providing vision, hope, and guidance. Authentic communication is people-centric and values-based, and includes compassion and understanding.

I work with women in leadership, business owners, and executives who are ready to expedite their growth, thereby accelerating their careers and growing their businesses.

My clients often struggle with staff turnover when they're starting, finding themselves to be constantly putting out fires, appeasing conflicts in personality, motivating unengaged employees, squashing poor listening skills and lack of critical thinking, and making up for missed deadlines. Here, micromanaging is happening, and there is an overall lack of trust and lack of ownership present, with everyone finger-pointing and blaming each other for the lack of results. There's a desire to expand the company, yet the leadership required within the team to carry out such an expansion is lacking.

My own journey of trauma, survival, growth and ultimately thriving has allowed me to really hone in on what our clients need and deliver it in a proficient and effective way to achieve the very best results. My clients unleash their leadership potential, both for themselves and their team. Authentic communication, whereby they come to understand the various personality styles and how to modify their approach to communicating and connecting with them (in turn reducing conflicts and strengthening bonds) is learned.

Essentially, my focus is on the needs of my clients' teams, and involves delegation skills, active listening, coaching employees, and building each team's collaboration so higher productivity is attained. Users are also guided through the process of putting together a specific hiring process to ensure our clients are able to hire and retain top talent, align job descriptions with employee strengths, and create a growth environment built on trust. Sales training is additionally up for grabs, in turn achieving higher profits. In this way, employees engage more, resulting in higher productivity.

Now, in stark contrast to the life I was living decades ago, my days are marked by meeting with a client's senior management team, completing preliminary assessments to help identify the business's blind spots, and providing executive coaching for senior leaders. Consulting services are also presented in mind of addressing the possibility of process reengineering or the creation of a hiring system for key positions, including benchmarking skills and creating interview assessments and unique questions for each applicant. Team workshops are also available if needed. Furthermore, our clients are provided with a comprehensive company leadership development plan tailored to their company's needs to help them grow their people, establish strong processes, and ultimately grow their profits. Moreover, through executive coaching, I also work to discover and identify any limiting beliefs and accordingly address them; reframing experiences and discovering truth, in turn creating positive beliefs to replace those that could potentially hold progress back.

In addition, individual and group work, offered either online or in person, has proven to be a particularly productive and needle-moving approach for my clients. These models allow me to direct my skillset and experience to helping my clients to grow at their pace, enhance their business, and expand their capacity—and the recognition that this is now my reality, which couldn't be more different to the life I once knew while still in survival mode, is something really special.

John Maxwell has been an authority in the leadership sector for more than forty years, and if he's taught me anything in the twenty years or so that he's been mentoring me for, it's that *teaching is ultimately serving*. Hence, I am here to help you to build trust and effective communication; I am here to equip you with the tools you'll use to start a movement of leading with love in your business—regardless of your circumstances or starting point.

Again, I love what I do—transforming people and organizations in a way that subsequently shapes families, communities, and the world as a whole.

Contact Candace

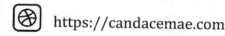 https://candacemae.com

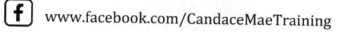 www.facebook.com/CandaceMaeTraining

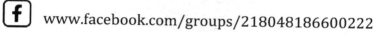 www.facebook.com/groups/218048186600222

 www.linkedin.com/in/candacemaegruber

 https://twitter.com/CandaceMae_com

✉ candace@candacemae.com

Candace's Resources

3 Christian Values That Will Double Your Profits:
https://go.candacemae.com

11 Ways Christian Leaders Can End Toxic Workplace
Cultures:
https://guide.candacemae.com

LORI TRULL

Optimal Wellness Performance Coach

ONE OF MY EARLIEST memories is of my mother putting on makeup in her bathroom.

I was sitting on the top of the closed toilet seat with my legs crossed, five years old, a tiny, freckled speck of a girl, trying to make sense of what I had just heard. My father had been away for a year, deployed overseas for the military, and my mom had been struggling to hold herself together while taking care of me and my little sister. In this memory, I can still feel the walls of the bathroom closing in on me as my mom explained how she didn't love us anymore; that when my daddy got home, we were done as a family. All I remember is hearing that my mother didn't love *me* anymore.

I never got the chance to sit down with my mom about that memory and ask what she remembers about that day. Regardless, I carried in my subconscious what I heard that day through many years of my life and derived one simple belief from it: I was not worthy of love.

In the years that followed, we lived with my dad and he remarried. We became a new, blended family, all with our own stories and traumas, trying to make our way in the world.

Throughout my childhood, I only saw my mother a few times a year until I was a teen. I learned over time that mental illness permeated her existence. There was a hole in my heart as I tried to bond with a woman who just wasn't capable of being a mother—and that hole led me to study psychology in college. The intellectual side of my brain wanted to understand; the child in me wanted to be loved, in turn seeking to connect with and feel loved by others—a drive that led me to naively accepting codependent "love" as validation for my worthiness.

I ended up marrying at twenty-one years old—way too young to know what I wanted in life and desperate for approval and love. My husband was also twenty-one and came with his own baggage that included substance abuse, his own self-doubt, and his own battle with worthiness—only his manifested in the form of an abusive, controlling power trip. Caught in a web with trying to make my way in the world while married to a man who very slowly worked to control everything in my life, I was still trying to find a way to make peace with my relationship with my mom.

Then, my life turned upside-down when she suddenly passed away as a result of a heart attack. She was only forty-seven; I was only twenty-three.

The depth to which that event rattled me took years for me to fully comprehend. For that first year after her death, I was in a really dark place: my marriage was so unhealthy, and after a miscarriage and two other deaths in my family in the six months that followed the passing of my mom, I divorced my husband and was walking through life numb and confused. My depression sank deeper, and on the anniversary of my mom's passing, I hit such a low place to the point where I just didn't want to be alive anymore. My rock bottom moment came in the middle of the night, when I lay in the middle of a dark road, praying for a car to just come by. I can still feel the roughness of the road and the heat from the ground contrasted with the cooler, damp night air. I wasn't even capable of crying at that point: numb had become my default.

As I lay there and looked at the night sky, my mind

having at this point been consumed for weeks regarding how I could just end everything, I said out loud, "I just don't want to be here anymore." As the tears flowed, I heard a voice—as clear as if someone was standing right there over me—that said, "You are meant to be here."

You are meant to be here.

Me? I thought.

I asked out loud, "Why? What am I supposed to do? How do I go on? How do I fix all this?"

I got no answers then. The voice—the message—was silent.

But deep inside me, I knew that it was the truth.

So, I got up off the street and started on a path to healing that would initially take me into days so much darker and painful than what had brought me to that moment—and yet I was changed from that point forward. I still had so much to learn, but that message had struck a chord deep inside me. *You are meant to be here.*

Months later, I got pregnant, remarried my ex-husband, and was now immersed and tangled in the web of alcoholism and emotional and verbal abuse that, over time, extended to abuse of every kind. Even still, I had a knowing that nothing could eclipse my newfound clarity; that I was *meant* to be here. Early on in the pregnancy I learned that while I was originally pregnant with twins, only one fetus was developing. Another loss, but I clung onto the hope the single child I was carrying now was also meant to be here.

I had my son in the spring of 2000, delivered into the world four weeks early. The end of my pregnancy was peppered with issues, and culminated when I had an eclamptic seizure. The signs were all there that the father to my son was back to his old ways and that I was on this journey alone.

The message that kept me going was that I was meant to be here.

The more I repeated that message in my head, the more I trusted it and the more I started to explore *how* I wanted to show up in the world: if I was meant to be here, then I was meant to *do* something—but what?

For nearly a decade from that point, I was a stay-at-home mom to my profoundly gifted son. Indeed, very quickly, parenting with the message *you are meant to be here* became my focus. I immersed myself in motherhood, sheltering my child from anything other than him knowing that he was meant to be here too.

Meanwhile, my husband's verbal, emotional, psychological, and physical abuse grew over the years, as did his drinking—but even in the midst of codependency, I was working on myself. I dug back into my psychology education and began exploring yoga more deeply. As a teenager, I had had the opportunity to stay at an ashram for a summer vacation, and I believe the door had opened for me to hear the message in the middle of the road that night. Yoga, meditation, and science merged for me and all intertwined into "we are meant to be here."

I began reading and studying with a voracious appetite from great philosophers and spiritual teachers, from the Tao Te Ching, yogic philosophy, Dr. Wayne Dyer, Neville Goddard, Abraham, A Course in Miracles, and so many others. I began to embody and understand on a cellular level that the message I had received was not just for me; it was for *everyone*. Hence, I meditated, journaled, and learned to trust the inner guidance that was growing. My heart had answers; I just needed to create space to hear them.

I began to shift, in the midst of abuse, to not seeing myself as a victim but looking for the lesson in it all. I began to form gratitude for the contrast I was experiencing; to see my abuser as someone that was also meant to be here, in this moment, for *me* to learn something. I began to see the web of it all entangled in a way that no longer felt overwhelming because I was shifting into a space of responsibility.

Notably, responsibility often gets conflated with blame: we often, as a protective mechanism to our own story, allow ourselves to sit in the energy of being a victim because what has happened to us wasn't our fault. While I do believe that—the abuse my husband was inflicting on me was not my fault, whether that be the rape, verbal arrows, psychological games, financial abuse, or physical threats—in meditating, ruminating, and processing over the course of a decade the message that saved my life, I realized that, yes, I *was* meant to be here. And that meant I had to take responsibility for *my* choices. It took several years for me to test out decisions, actions, mental frameworks, and mindsets to understand where my power truly was.

I came to realize that *I had choice*. Even when it looked like at every turn there were no choices in the external world, I realized my internal story was where all the power was. By shifting to gratitude for the contrast I was being shown and by being determined to take responsibility for my thoughts and actions, the world around me began to change.

I was in such a dramatic situation—one with an alcoholic abuser—that the shift took a few years and was truly pivotal, and while it got even darker and heavier in the process, I *knew* I was on the right path. I moved into a space of seeing everything with love and gratitude and with a wisdom that came from beyond me—not from a "Pollyanna Toxic Positivity" standpoint, but rather with a divine grace that recognized that, truly, the only way out was through love and gratitude.

I knew I was not meant to be here to suffer; I knew I was not meant to raise my son—a boy so wise beyond his years—to witness me being beaten by his father. I knew I was worthy of love, and the life of contrast I was living was a powerful teacher. I knew that there was power in the experience and that I was meant to be here to learn from all of that; that I was meant to grow and emerge on the other side with the message for others that, indeed, *you* are meant to be here. We *all* are meant to be here. I believe with every fiber of my being that there is greatness inside each and every one of us; it just gets buried under stories and beliefs that are laid on to our identities from childhood and throughout our lives.

To go back to my narrative, however, my marriage eventually erupted in a catalyzing moment: after weeks of terrorizing me, my husband delivering bouts of daily abuse, from shoving and choking to extreme gaslighting and mental and emotional abuse lasting hours and hours—sometimes all night—his rage culminated into one defining moment. In the spring of 2009, I was asleep on the couch, early in the morning, the sun not even up yet, when he threw on all of the lights and began shouting, trying to shake me awake with his rage. This was a common tactic, like a terrorist rattling you at your most vulnerable state so the nervous system is in complete disarray. I refused to engage, as I tried so often to do; I just closed my eyes and said we would talk later.

Moments after that, I was struck in the face with a toolbox that he had thrown across the room at my head.

A toolbox that became the final straw.

This was the moment when my message so loudly showed up and said, *You are meant to be here, and now you are finally ready to go to the next phase of your life journey.*

The moment of culmination of all the lessons and work I had undergone; of my not losing myself in that marriage; of my preparation for the long journey ahead.

While he was in jail for the incident of that weekend, I packed up what I could, took my son, and went into hiding. The subsequent eighteen-month court battle for custody and a divorce all interwoven with the criminal case meant my world was in such disarray that I had brief moments of wondering how it was going to all work out—and yet that voice that had spoken to my core—*you are meant to be here*—was also saying to me now, "If you go back to him, you will not be alive to live the life you are meant to live. You are ready now to do this. The world needs you. Keep going. Do not give up. Trust in love and gratitude."

And so I did while remaining grateful at every turn for the enormous challenges. I found a way to see every single insurmountable issue as a gift, and, miraculously, the situations always ended up having a solution. Here commenced a journey where even though we were penniless, homeless, and living in fear for my life, what my son and I needed *always* showed up.

I learned that my responsibility was to control every single thought I had. My responsibility was to own my narrative; my responsibility was to see everything through the lens of gratitude. And while this can seem esoteric, this is grounded deep in neuroscience: the beliefs we hold are the filter from which we see the world. There is no objective reality; every single experience is unique to the observer as a result of their vantage point, bias, and beliefs. And the brain, filtering through four hundred billion bits of information in any given second, seeks to validate that initial thought that you hold. So if I had decided that leaving that life of abuse was too hard or impossible and that I would never be able to make it with no money and him in control of everything external, then my brain would have only shown me how it was, in fact, impossible. And yet as a result of my studies, application, and exploration of the mind and the power of the story we tell ourselves, I took responsibility and owned the lens; I chose to see it all as a lesson, every challenge acting as a contrast; as a teacher. I chose to be grateful and to seek solutions—and because of that lens, solutions always appeared.

The path to freedom was always inside me, just as it is inside you.

I know without a doubt there is no "out there" in terms of our problems: it is not the other person; it is not the relationship; it is not the system; it is not *anything* outside of us. It is how we are choosing to see and feel about what we are experiencing.

Freedom is one hundred percent in our control, since we are creating our experiences by holding a narrative; by telling a story that only lets us see things in alignment with that story. Confirmation bias is like a goat walking down a well-worn path, with each thought we have acting like a goat walking the paths we have built with our story. From a simple thought of seeing water in a glass to holding an opinion about another person, what we *think* we see is what we see—and those thoughts are a powerful filter.

The goats love to walk the same path over and over and over again, and many of them have been walked our entire life—so to the unaware, the thoughts just follow the path they always have. However, through awareness, you can begin to see the patterns of your story.

That is where I always start with my clients and students: with becoming aware. As a coach, I hold space for others to explore where all the goats in their brain are going. Do they run down that well-worn path right into the snake pit—the pit of anxiety and worry and overwhelm and unworthiness?

This is extremely common in the world; I see it so often. People's thoughts and beliefs are running on autopilot with no awareness—but by creating awareness, it opens the door for possibility.

Possibility. It is so powerful. I truly believe anything is possible, and I have lived out that belief fully! I went from homeless, penniless, on food stamps, and living in fear for my life as a single mom raising a profoundly gifted child in the midst of trauma and abuse, to a successful businesswoman and entrepreneur. Not only have I grown my coaching business to impact lives for people to reach optimal performance and happiness in their lives, but I am also a successful corporate consultant for one of the world's largest software companies.

I have traveled the world, bought a boat, built financial stability and wealth, fallen in love with a true partner, and, most importantly, fallen in love with myself. I have healed my heart; my mind; my story; my life. I found that it didn't matter what my mother said to me when I was five because I could change the narrative and decide that she loved me as best as *she* could. Healing *me* was the only work I needed to do.

I successfully got full custody of my son and raised him to be a caring, emotionally intelligent, loving person despite the trauma and tragedy he witnessed growing up. And because of every challenge life has graced me with, I have taken every lesson and learned to thrive—and, in turn, have built my coaching model around this. My trademarked programming, Conscious Consumption®, operates on the foundation that when we become conscious of everything we consume, we sit in the seat of power in our lives.

Every thought, every movement, every meal, either regenerates our energy or depletes it. Our lives are built as a series of tiny moments; tiny decisions; tiny habits, over and over, that if done unconsciously, are the goats just treading down the well-worn path. And to change our lives, we have to start with *us*; with what we are doing, thinking, and, most importantly, believing and *feeling*.

We all have challenges, and in many ways, each and every one of us has experienced trauma. Sometimes, this is as Earth-shattering as losing a mother you are still trying to make peace with suddenly at a young age, or a flying toolbox smacking you in the face; other times, it is subtle moments of trauma that layer on and feed the demon of unworthiness, shame, or feeling unlovable. Regardless, it doesn't matter how big the challenge or the trauma; the pain we hold is still the same—and my mission and goal for impact in the world is to help as many people as I can to shed that pain so they can live a life of freedom.

We all deserve love and the space to shine in the world—each and every one of us. Hence, through merging yoga, optimal nutrition, neuroscience, mindset, HeartMath™, and several other modalities, I work with individuals and groups to uncover that greatness. I don't believe that anything is missing in our lives, nor do I believe that we need to seek answers outside us: I believe we hold all the answers we need. But to hear the answers and our truth, we have to remove the crap that keeps us stuck in a narrative that doesn't serve us. Such a truth and message emerges when we bring awareness, Conscious Consumption®, and clarity to our life.

We have no limitations: we can choose to walk the goats down another path—the one to possibility. If we let our thoughts roam and wander without awareness and direction, they always find their way back to the well-worn road, and that has never served any of us well; it *always* leads to the same outcome. The new outcomes come from new paths, stories, and beliefs, and the power of possibility lies in this process.

Wellness through wisdom starts with the heart, and the journey to the truth leads us to our center; to the heart; to wisdom. My job as a coach is to hold space for such exploration to ask questions and to share observations to allow you to hear your own answers.

Our clients have come to us struggling with health or weight, financial issues, relationships, physical pain, lack of accomplishment toward goals, frustration in building a business or professional success, and many other limiting stories. Through Conscious Consumption®, personal coaching, and our Exquisite Life Lab group coaching, our clients have emerged free and empowered toward their goals in every facet of their lives. The tools and programs we provide create true results: rather than just education and philosophy and theory, we teach exactly how to get the goats off the well-worn path and onto that new direction you want your life to go in. And when you begin to own that process, become aware, and become equipped with actionable tools to create change, moment to moment, you begin to achieve the life you want. You become changed, and you emerge as the best version of you, creating a ripple effect around you as you do so. Your commitment to taking full responsibility in your life and owning your story gives others around you permission to begin doing the same thing. The emergence expands; it is inevitable.

This is my passion: to be the catalyst for change. I believe in you because *you* are meant to be here. *I* am meant to be here. *We* are meant to be here.

Emergent You was founded on that mission: to infuse love and gratitude into every moment and to impact the world by holding space for the emergence of everyone we come into contact with.

We work with individuals, small groups, corporate programing, leaders, and entrepreneurs, and while we already have many programs in place, we also create custom programming for groups and businesses. Creating resilience and coherence at the individual level expands into teams and leaders to influence impactful growth in any organization.

To run the best business, to have the healthiest team, and to have the happiest family, *you* must show up in every moment as the best version of you.

The **you** that is *meant to be here* is waiting to emerge, and I'm here to help and guide you, so that you can be fully and inexcusably *you*.

Contact Lori

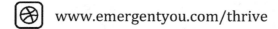 www.emergentyou.com/thrive

[f] www.facebook.com/listentolori

[f] www.facebook.com/groups/925783444433241

[in] www.linkedin.com/in/lorilpalmer

[ⓞ] www.instagram.com/yogilorilume

[✉] lori@illuminateenterprises.com

Lori's Resources

Clarity Call:
www.emergentyou.com/thrive

FELICITY BUDDIG

Founder & CEO of *She Is You* and High-Performance Coach

THERE I WAS, CURLED up on my mom's bedroom floor, playing with my dollhouse—the one my mother made me for Christmas. I was an imaginative ten-year-old girl, and I quickly learned I could escape my reality of dysfunction, neglect, and abuse by creating a home for my bear family that was loving, safe, clean, and full of hope.

Growing up in a deeply dysfunctional and toxic family, I had no chance of thriving, especially considering the terrible upper respiratory issues I had faced since infancy. From the moment of that diagnosis, I was nicknamed Wheeze—and Wheeze was swiftly groomed into a young woman consumed by doubt, failure, unworthiness, and complete hopelessness. We mirror what we know as kids, young adults and so forth, and for myself, I witnessed my father's attempt at killing my mother when I was ten. My upbringing was one of conditional love, dysfunction, chaos, and mental and emotional abuse. By the time I hit young adulthood, I felt I had zero chance of growing into the successful woman I used to imagine being when I would play with my Barbie; instead, I dropped out of high school, deeply depressed, and was left with no direction in life. I experienced intense thoughts of suicide in pursuit of ending my decades-long battle with hopelessness.

Indeed, the lack of support and role models I had had in my family led me to fall into the arms of an abuser as a young adult: I fell head over heels for him—a moment that would lead to the relationship that would ultimately teach me the hardest life lessons. He was my escape; he gave me freedom from my ever-pervading feeling of hopelessness. He swooped right in and showered me with promises of *I can't be without you* and *I love you*— words I had craved for my entire life. I was hooked!

My ex-husband was the first man to show interest in my world: he wanted to explore everything about me, inside and out. However, there was trouble in Paradise:

what ignited our spark and brought us together were two lost souls filling a void.

Our sexual chemistry was intense and amazing, forming the ignition in our relationship—meaning, before I knew it, we were having a baby. Everything was happening so fast; we had only met a few months before.

He was excited and calm, but deep down inside, my fear paralyzed me. Thoughts riddled with doubt flooded my head: *Do I want to be with him? What will my family say?* The uncertainty I felt was overwhelming.

When we told his family, they were welcoming and excited, while mine ridiculed me and beat me emotionally, my mother turning her back on me by kicking me out of the house. I wouldn't deal with the fallout of this abandonment until much later down the road, but at the time, I was heartbroken and orphaned. I felt robbed of the joy that women typically experience with their first baby—something that was stolen from me by my mother turning her back.

My pregnancy was hard, and it challenged my health to the point where I was told I couldn't have any more children after I lost my second child due to severe complications. This was the beginning of many life-threatening obstacles I would have to endure in my marriage.

Regardless, my son was born a beautiful, healthy boy, and, for a time, I was a stay-at-home mom. On the outside, everything looked pretty good, but behind closed doors, things were dark, dangerous, and extremely life-threatening: my then-husband was a full-fledged raging alcoholic, which deepened my childhood wounds of self-worth, uselessness, and feelings of hopelessness. He controlled everything I did, down to the pennies I spent at the grocery store. I would eventually seek solace through suicidal ideations yet again, sensing that this was my only way to freedom after a good decade of living this nightmare, day in and day out.

*

In February 2013, my father passed away. As I sat beside my mother in her final hours, I still can't wrap my head around the fact that I lost both my parents as little as three months apart. The derelict house my mother had raised us in was going to be gone forever. Where would I escape to in the middle of the night when my husband was in a drunken rage, pulling me out of our bed? Despite their shortcomings, my parents had been my safety net.

I needed a plan—and quick.

February to August was a complete whirlwind: we sold both my parents' homes, and I convinced my now-ex to purchase a house across the street from my little brother. This new home was Part One of my plan and would keep my son and I safe when things turned ugly.

In the course of one full year, I buried my parents, sold three homes, and began to map out my exit plan to leave my then-husband. Why? Because I knew that, if I were to stay with him, I would wind up dead. Abusive partners destroy every ounce of self-esteem, worth, and confidence in their partner—plus, his financial abuse meant that, if I was really going to leave him, I was going to need a job, as well as the courage to leap.

My spirituality was non-existent at this point: I grew up Catholic and attended Mass, but I felt no real connection to a bigger source; rather, I felt as though God had abandoned me, since my entire life had been one continuous cycle of abuse.

Saying this, I started to explore meditation when I discovered reiki healing. Meditation opened my eyes, while reiki gave me the understanding that we hold the power to change. That Level One Reiki class was life-altering for me: it was the catalyst I needed to stand in my power. The hopeless victim role I had held onto would fade away, and the words *nothing is impossible* would begin to drive me. The fog began to dissipate, and

I finally began to feel worthy and deserving of the life that that little ten-year-old girl had imagined when she would play with her dollhouse.

I had one plan, and that was to become the woman I was always meant to be. My vision was to create a life of safety for my son and I.

With this incentive in mind, I began to work on myself when my son and then-husband were away at school and work respectively. This was prime time for me to dive headfirst into affirmations and meditating. I had notecards hidden throughout the house that I would repeat daily:

I am capable of doing great things.
I am worthy of the life I create.
I am loved.
I am beautiful.

I built a vision board and tucked it away in a closet, and I would meditate in front of it, allowing the vibes and good thoughts that ran through my head to come to life.

Slowly but surely, I began to turn my pain into power. I also started to recognize that my life path and purpose was to help other women in similar circumstances. My eyes were opening to a whole world of possibilities.

My faith was at the forefront of my making everything possible; it was certainly becoming the foundation of my life.

As I grew mentally stronger, I found that my vision of me leaving was slowly becoming my reality. Now, all I needed was a job. I had spent twenty-two years in the veterinary industry, my passion for animals and helping people allowing me to acquire a good reputation.

After countless online searches for positions in this field that were close to home, however, I was once again feeling hopeless. I prayed daily for a job.

It was during one morning when I was on the phone to my girlfriend crying, "I will never break free from him," sinking in my sorrow, that I received a Facebook message from a mutual friend at a clinic I called on frequently. The message read, *Felicity, it's Mel. Would you happen to be looking for a job?*

Of course, my response was a resounding yes: this was everything I had prayed for, since it was close to home and offered family-friendly hours. The pay, however, was minimum wage, but that didn't stop me from taking the position. This meant I was one step closer to my escape!

I was on Cloud Nine—and then reality hit: my husband wanted my earnings to pay the bills.

I felt utterly hopeless, and this theme of "one step forward, two steps back" would be a reoccurring pattern throughout my journey. It would challenge me harder each time I grew closer to escaping, as my ex's energy constantly pushing back that much stronger each time.

*

Fast-forward some time, and I was making progress. I had found a home to rent nearby, and I would take thirty dollars from each pay cycle to buy things to set a foundation for the life I would be building; four sets of silverware here, four bath towels here, dishes in between. I had arranged for movers to come while my husband was at work and shared none of this with him or my son out of fear of word getting out.

The day we moved out, Chicago was hit with a huge ice storm, and I was fearful that the movers would cancel—but they made it. The two men that arrived had no idea what they were getting into: I sat there sobbing out of fear and relief upon their approval, and walked away with a small loveseat, armoire, end tables, and a multitude of other things that had been donated to me. I had no idea what challenges I would face; I was riding on my faith, and put my trust in the belief that God would continue to guide us.

Over the course of the next several years, I would face life-altering challenges that had the potential to send me back into the arms of my ex. However, I stood strong.

Reality hit when I realized I had only forty-five dollars to my name and needed to buy groceries. Undeterred, however, I hustled like there was no tomorrow for the first two years after our move, working two or three jobs at a time. I was always just one paycheck away from losing everything. When I look back, I wonder how my son and I survived my losing my job for four months, our power being cut off, our having an empty fridge, the crippling divorce debt, and having no health insurance. Regardless, we were safe and happy: no matter how difficult it was, we managed to pull through every time.

During this time, I worked on letting go of my emotional attachment to my ex. Indeed, the full extent of this trauma would be unpacked much later down the road. My visions and desires were also growing at this stage, just waiting to be brought to fruition. I was about to embark on a journey of a lifetime.

Ultimately, what began as a daydream for this once-overweight, hopeless, and lost woman is now my reality: I overcame a ton, surviving a dysfunctional childhood, emotional and mental abuse from my family, depression, anxiety, obesity, and self-doubt. I was moments away from ending my life at multiple points in my life, praying to God all the way to take my pain away. I was beyond broke and burdened with a large amount of debt that almost led me to lose my house and car.

What saved me was my faith: in these moments of despair, I gripped onto my faith, prayed hard, and meditated on peace and abundance. Even though life was physically hard for me, spiritually, I always maintained the energy of abundance and fertility in my consciousness. I worked hard and eventually began to reap the benefits from it: I went from being a part-time reiki practitioner to a full-time high-performance coach for seven-figure midlife women in business. I now mentor women in my Chicagoland home and am the founder of *She Is You*, an online magazine for women in their forties and fifties. Our growing social media platform is dedicated to supporting women through their midlife awakening by focusing on the four pillars of life (spirituality, health/wellness, career/business, and relationships). After all, regardless of whether you're a lost woman with no clue what her life purpose is or the high-functioning Type A CEO woman who is exhausted popping phentermine for energy, we are all one and the same, just packaged a little differently. Irrespective of income, status, education, and money, problems are problems, and high-achieving women share the exact same issues as middle-class women; the difference is that, while one is wrapped up in Gucci, the other is in Michael Kors!

My clients seek me out because they are feeling "unsatisfied" in some way or another. From that point, I work with them one-on-one for six weeks—if not longer—unpacking the uncomfortable and really getting to the root of their definition of being "unsatisfied" or a "failure". Once this has been identified, we can work together on identifying their triggers—what caused this derailment/these bad habits—and begin working on introducing healthier habits and boundaries, ultimately allowing them to walk away feeling much more balanced, connected to the relationships that matter most, and focused on what is important to them in life.

I have worked with women just like myself, who are starting with nothing more than the clothes on their backs, guiding them via my mentorship through their own rebuilding of their lives and helping them to confront their own feelings of unworthiness, disconnectedness, burnout, self-sabotage all the while.

Victory feels like a bottle of champagne being poured through your veins: every ounce of yourself is pulsating with this warm, bubbly feeling.

Over the years, I can honestly say that I have conquered the beast—the beast being my previously negative state of mind. When I tasted freedom for the first time without the burden of my ex, I became unstoppable, and what I recognized was that the people that may be "closest" to you are, in fact, often the ones putting you down. This is a hard reality to face, but it's been a humble one also, and ultimately gave me the courage to walk away from all the toxic relationships present in my family. This was something I simply had to do if I wanted a real chance of growing into the woman I was meant to be!

I have pulled myself through the fire all my life, and am finally free to really stand in my power—and it feels fucking amazing! Growth is ugly and painful, but so is staying stuck due to fear of the unknown. I may not have fully completed my education, but what I lack in textbook diplomas I excel in common sense, ability to think outside the box, and self-belief.

Over the past seven or so years, I have accomplished more than most do throughout their entire lives: I have written my memoir and launched a magazine for all of you ladies to help and support you on your journey. I am building a successful coaching practice and online community, and have also taken this past year to unpack forty-four years of trauma. This by far has been the hardest obstacle for me to conquer, but God grew my strength over time through the death of my parents, my divorce, and giving my own son the gift of healing away from me. I have had to do many hard things, and because of that, victory is in my veins.

I am grateful for my second chance at life.

Indeed, my unconventional method of success has allowed me to use these very same techniques with my clients. I will not offer you a step-by-step coaching package; rather, what I *will* do is get you in the zone where you begin to tap into your spirituality and ground yourself. From there, we can begin to explore the four pillars of a midlife woman's life. Indeed, my six-week course is designed to do exactly this.

Meanwhile, my mentorship program is something I open up to very specific women that are really ready to do the big work; the transformation. This is a journey that can last anywhere from six months to one year—if not longer.

So, I ask all of you to really dig deep and ask yourself: Are you ready to conquer your beast? Are you willing to face your fears and do hard things? Are you ready to become the woman you are meant to be?

Xo,
Felicity Nicole

Contact Felicity

https://sheisyoumag.com

www.facebook.com/SheIsYouMag

www.facebook.com/groups/sheisyoucommunity

www.instagram.com/sheisyoumag

felicitybuddig@gmail.com

JENNI VIKEN

Breakthrough & Life Coach

I AM A SURVIVOR of domestic violence.

I grew up as a people-pleaser, feeling unworthy; I looked to others for validation, and when it came to any relationship I would get into, I was dependent on them and how they saw me. This resulted in my being in unhealthy relationships for the majority of my life.

I had my first encounter with physical abuse when I was sixteen, which occurred at the hands of my first serious boyfriend. We got into an argument, and I wanted to leave. I was at the top of the stairs. He was mad and gave me a shove. I went tumbling down the stairs and he came running down, saying how sorry he was. He started crying and telling me how much he loved me; that he only got upset because I had said I was going to leave, which had made him panic.

I hugged him and said it was okay. We watched a movie to make up.

I loved the attention he gave me for the next few hours after the attack—the kind of attention abusers typically use to keep you from leaving. They do so to get you to believe they only do crazy stuff because they "love you so much".

A few days later, my boyfriend got mad when I brought up our fight: I showed him some bruises I had from the fall and he got really upset. "I *told* you I'm sorry. How many times are you going to throw this in my face?"

I felt sick to my stomach and quickly learned that it wasn't going to be okay to talk about this with him ever again.

His controlling behaviors got progressively worse and, after a few months, I broke it off with him. I felt relieved—until I found out he liked another girl. For some reason, my crazy brain told me to write him a letter begging him to take me back. Thankfully, he chose not to.

Sadly, that was just my first of what would become several unhealthy relationships.

For the next two years, I dated one broken boy after

another until the point I got married and found myself in an abusive relationship for many years. Neither of us had been shown an example of a healthy relationship growing up, and we didn't have at our disposal any of the tools for building one. I lacked self-confidence and looked to him for validation, receiving abuse instead—a combination that resulted in a toxic environment for many years.

During our sixteen years of marriage, we had three children together, all two years apart. I thought at the time that things had started okay, but, looking back, the red flags were definitely there—and there were more than just a few.

Regardless, I didn't know what I didn't know: I didn't know that abuse typically starts with isolation—isolating you from your friends and family by making up lies about them and putting crazy ideas into your head regarding how they're "not good for you".

It wasn't just with me, however; it was the kids as well. He became very controlling of where they went and who they could go with, and would make me lie or make excuses to my family about why they couldn't spend time alone with the kids. I didn't know what gaslighting was at the time, so when he twisted and turned everything around on me, I thought I was the one with the problem. I thought if I could be better—a better mom by keeping the kids quieter and the house cleaner; by working harder and making more money—then things would be better. I didn't know that the silent treatment also constituted abuse. He would go days—even weeks—without talking to me as a punishment for something that I had done to upset him. We were all walking on eggshells, not knowing how he was going to act or when he was going to be upset. This is also abuse.

Then, there was the intimidation, delivered via certain looks (glares) and gestures. The worst for me was when he would yell really close to my face, his finger pointing at me (but careful to not touch it); so close I could almost feel it. I hated that; it scared me so much. The look he had in his eyes when he was mad is something I will never forget.

Unlike the other behaviors or abusive traits, I knew this one wasn't right, along with the obsessive control and verbal abuse I endured.

To make matters worse, he got really good at putting on a show in public: he made sure to participate not only in community activities but also in coaching the kids in sports. Everybody seemed to like him: he was friends with everyone—even the cops in our town—so you can imagine that, when I challenged or confronted him, he would say things like, "Nobody will believe you," or, "No judge will ever give you custody of the kids. You might not get to see them at all."

I began to believe these things to be true, and even though I hated my life and knew that this was doing extreme damage to my children, I felt as though there was no way out. I blamed myself for a lot of it, which wasn't helped by the fact that none of what we had been through was ever justified to us by others as not being okay: friends and family saw this different side of our life, his family seeing the most—including a lot of things that weren't right—but when they would speak about it, they would say things that would make it even worse, like, "Hopefully the kids can settle/quiet down and let him rest," or, "He's under a lot of stress." In a nutshell, they would never acknowledge his abusive behavior. I believe this was due to the fact that this behavior is what they knew to be standard in their own family; we all know that abuse is generational, so, of course, they didn't see an issue with it.

As the icing on the cake, my leaving felt all the more impossible considering the fact we had multiple bankruptcies, outstanding debt, and a low credit score—plus, my name was on both vehicles and all of the bills were in my name. I had no idea how I would ever recover.

One day, however, the tide turned.

I returned home from work, and instantly I knew something was off with him. What I didn't know was that this day would change everything for my children and I, and as sad as it sounds, it was just the thing I needed to get out.

He had had a fight with our middle son, which ended with my son pinned on the bed and his threatening to kill him. One thing led to another and, before I knew it, I had been punched in the face so hard that I literally flew across the room. It wasn't the first time things had been physical, but it was the first time it had happened directly in front of the kids. Sadly, in a very sick way, this was exactly what I needed to happen: although I feel that physical abuse is nothing compared to the coercive control abusers use over and over again, and although I would do things very differently if I could go back, this event gave me the power and justification to start the process to leave—but, just to be sure, God gave me a few more situations to help the process along.

A few days after this event, my daughter and I were driving in the car together (she was nine) when she looked over at me and she said, "I am so proud of you, Mom." I was shocked: our life was so bad; I had no idea what she could possibly be proud of me for. So I asked her why, and she said, "Because you did such a good job of covering up that bruise on your face."

This was the lowest of the low; the worst feeling a mom could ever feel. I pulled over and started to cry, and at that moment, I knew I couldn't do this any longer; that this was what I was teaching my daughter; that this was what she looked up to me for. I was experiencing the worst shame and guilt, and, from that moment, I made it a priority to find a place for the kids and I to live.

To top it off, a few days later, at my daughter's hockey practice, somebody almost nonchalantly said to me, "You know, this doesn't seem right." It wasn't much, but it was everything I needed to tip the scales; to help me to realize, *Oh, wow, this* really *isn't right.*

From that point, I started to do one thing better: I began personal development and learned to value myself without needing the validation of others. Because of this change, I am now in a fantastic healthy relationship, with myself and with others. I went from feeling unworthy and dependent on others to worthy and independent.

What did I see in my future that encouraged me to take the leap of faith? Health, safety, and freedom of choice.

After doing the hard work on myself, identifying my core values, and working on integrity in all areas of my life, I attracted the most amazing man. We dated, got married, and the kids and I moved in with him. Everything was good. We both also had good jobs. I had worked with large pharma and medical device companies for my entire adult life. I liked my job and thought I would stay there until I retired.

I started to work on my credit and to pay off bills, the kids were okay... and yet something was missing. I really felt that I lacked passion and a purpose for my life. I was sad because I had created the life that I had always dreamed of, yet there was *something missing*. This remained unresolved until I completed a personal development challenge: I declared I wanted to write a book. To my surprise, my coach for this challenge said, "That's great. I happen to know a book-publishing coach. I will connect you tomorrow."

I was taken back at this, as I actually didn't know if I *could* write a book at that time. But there was this crazy tugging on my heart; I could barely sleep that night. I kept thinking about how hard I had worked to understand all types of abuse so that I would know for "next time" and be able to leave sooner—and yet, even after I had left that relationship, I was still insecure and feeling unworthy—until I started working on myself.

I started to think, *I wonder how many other women are like me; in these relationships and don't even know it.* How could this be a thing? How could all of these stories and what these men were saying all be the same?

Sure enough, I would awaken in the middle of the

night and receive downloads that I needed to tell my story; I had to help others who were where I used to be who didn't know this was a thing.

At first, I thought this would just take the form of my book; that I could write an easy book for women to read in one day in which I could sprinkle in my story as examples and teach them about gaslighting, narcissism, verbal and emotional control, manipulation, and all the other types of abuse.

As I was getting ready to launch my book, however, God was telling me that I needed to do more; that I needed to quit my job and help other women; that I needed to become a coach. He made it clear that my mission—my assignment—was to help women who had been in (and who continued to be in) unhealthy abusive relationships.

*

The difficulties; the uphill climbs; the lack of self-belief; the doubt; the insecurity; the lack of support (from your spouse; friends; family); the loneliness; the feeling of there being no end in sight or end of the tunnel; needing time to heal; the responsibility; the children.

In an abusive relationship, you dream about living a

life of peace, love, and respect; chances are, that is why you have stayed so long in the first place (and the second, third, and fourth place): you hoped and dreamed that things would change; that you could still have that life with him that you had dreamed of; that you were waiting for. You have seen weeks—and sometimes even months—of change and normalization take place, and this gives you hope—but, each and every time, you are faced with a letdown. Sometimes, it gradually comes back, to the point where you don't even really realize it; and other times, it just right-up slaps you in the face. Either way, it always comes back, and then you feel the shame and guilt that you fell for the same thing all over again.

I dreamed about the day I would be courageous enough to leave. I envisioned my kids and I living this peaceful, safe life where there wasn't any yelling and we never worried if someone was going to be mad or get upset. However, I quickly found out that that isn't exactly how it works; leaving was hard, but the following weeks, months and year were much harder than I had ever expected. I have learned now how important it is to set boundaries and stick to them; without them, nothing changes except the fact that you live in a different home. You see, when you are under their roof and they know where you are and what you're doing, they are okay—

but when you leave and they lose complete control, that is when you need to really be careful (and set boundaries, which I didn't do for over a year). You have made many threats before and haven't stuck to them, and so they now don't believe you; they think that you will fold. For me, this is where things got scary; where the stalking started. Take care of yourself and your children; set those boundaries and begin to cultivate a safe space for yourself. I did, and I am now the bestselling author of the book *Choosing Healthy Relationships: In Life, Wellness and Love*, a self-help book for identifying and overcoming abuse and how to move forward after. I am a certified breakthrough and life coach and real estate investor and am currently taking training to become a domestic violence advocate and a real estate agent. I have a future vision to purchase commercial properties and rent them out as transitional housing for women who cannot find a place to stay after leaving their abusive relationship.

Although I primarily help women who have previously been in unhealthy relationships (these are my paid clients), I also help women who are still in these relationships—just on a different level. In my free private Facebook group, these amazing women are able to get resources, support, and advice from me, in addition to the others in the group. I also provide a free weekly support group call (on Zoom), where I provide trainings on different topics around abuse and help answer any questions that might warrant immediate help. I let my clients know they are not isolated and alone; I let them not only understand that they have choices, but show that they can feel empowered to make the choices they know they need to make.

The goal is to take clients and help them to move forward to living an empowered and independent life, helping them to find validation from within so they no longer need to look to others to fulfill that for them.

To summarize, I help women who are feeling trapped, isolated, underconfident, as though they are the problem, and shameful and guilty, wondering how they could have let this happen; how did it get this bad?

What my own journey, coupled with me working with so many different women in similar situations, is that, even if it feels like it, you are not alone. It is the commonality of this narrative we tell ourselves that inspired me to create the wealth of resources available on my website, whether you need something to easily download and digest, or more tangible support, such as on a call or retreat.

First and foremost, my priority is centered on making sure all women in my orbit are safe, my goal being to help them realize that, if they feel something isn't right, it truly isn't (which my downloadable *10 Signs*

That You May Be In An Unhealthy Relationship can really help them to identify). My focus is then on helping those women to create the independent life they have always dreamed of; to help them to develop a healthy spiritual life, healthy relationships, and a healthy physical life for themselves. In this way, they will feel and look better than ever, find peace, be the role model they have always wanted to be, and recognize they are not unworthy, but strong, independent, and more than capable of creating the life they were made for.

I am proof that it is possible to go from feeling unworthy and broken in every way possible to creating the independent life of one's dreams.

I am proof that it's possible to finally break free.

I am proof that all women can do the same.

Contact Jenni

 www.jenniviken.com

 www.facebook.com/jenni.maxey.1

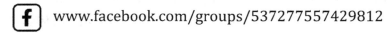

www.facebook.com/groups/537277557429812

www.linkedin.com/in/jenni-viken-1816848a

www.instagram.com/jenniviken

jennilviken@gmail.com

Jenni's Resources

Free Consultation:
https://calendly.com/jennilviken/connect

10 Signs You May Be in An Unhealthy Relationship:
www.jenniviken.com/product/choosing-healthy-relationships/

3-Month 1:1 Coaching:
www.jenniviken.com/product/3-month-11-breakthrough-coaching

6-Week Group Coaching:
www.jenniviken.com/product/6-week-group-coaching

DENISE CONDE

Life Coach

MY NAME IS DENISE Francine Conde and I was born on April 17, 1972, in a coal-dusted city outside of Buffalo, New York. When I was eighteen months old, my parents moved my two older sisters and I to a small riverside, picturesque village in Youngstown, New York, where I grew up.

In my mind at the time, I had a pretty normal childhood: my father was a Vietnam veteran, and I honor his story and his valor, even though, alongside millions of children of Vietnam veterans, I experienced physical and mental abuse from him as a byproduct of his PTSD from his time in the war. My father also suffered from alcoholism, which he overcame by the time I was ten years old. However, his fits of rage carried on in a cyclic pattern, reigning fear and terror until the time God brought him back home.

Despite everything I endured as a child, I was gifted with the absolute will and strength over my unresolved trauma to become a special education teacher. This proved to be a difficult journey, as alcohol and drugs became my coping mechanisms to drown out the unhealed pain from my childhood that I had repressed. I failed out of college and was constantly on the run, seeking safety and shelter—but even then, I didn't give up.

It took me eight years to get my bachelor's degree, become a special education teacher, and an additional five years to attain my master's degree, fighting against my being told that I would never become a teacher and that my master's degree was only a piece of paper from people who were supposed to support me all the while. I was soon honored with the blessing of my beautiful daughters, Grace and Maggie, and swore that my trauma would not become theirs—although while still in my first marriage, I noticed similar traits to the marriage of my parents: my husband and I would often fall into the uncomfortable familiarity of yelling, screaming, my infidelity, and disrespecting ourselves and one another. I blamed my ex-husband for all our problems and divorced him, refusing to look hard enough at myself and my own unresolved trauma, conditioning, and patterns to accept some responsibility. Now, I know that what you don't heal, you repeat—and yet at that point in time, I thought that I had forgiven my father long ago. However, it wasn't until I started recognizing the conditioning and patterns of my parents in my second marriage to Michael that I realized that I had pushed my true feelings of what he had put me through down, brushing them aside.

After my father's passing, my mother became someone I no longer recognized: narcissistic tendencies. She and my oldest sister would unleash her rage onto me any time she felt necessary, refusing to accept that she was anything other than a parent doing what she believed was best for her adult children.

As I started to implement boundaries with my mother and sister, my mother called Child Protective Services on me, claiming I was abusing alcohol and my daughters. This call forced me onto an unrelenting path of healing and threw me into situations in which I was forced to either sink or swim; to accept and truly move forward from what had happened to me; to heal from every traumatic event of my life or to face repeating the lessons.

In the midst of these events, Michael and I separated, during which time we agreed to work on ourselves. The deepest part of me that urged me to step into my power and pursue this journey was my family—my husband, Michael, and my girls. I knew if I didn't heal, my family couldn't, either.

My mother's calling Child Protective Services—the worst situation I had been in in my adult life, bar my father's passing—and the lack of control I had in that situation forced me to look at my life and the decisions I had made and how I was currently living compared to the person that my daughters and Michael deserved. This situation, perhaps counterintuitively, opened up a craving within me that desperately desired healing and to put an end to my mother's, father's, and oldest sister's endless abuse. I knew that not only did my family deserve better, but so did I. I knew that I was a good mother; I knew I was a good person to the core; and this event opened me up to the passion burning in my soul to let it all out; to stop playing a role and pretending I was okay to appease others. Instead of bringing me to my knees, I decided to rise with sheer will and determination. I took up the flag of healing and ran with it, becoming utterly vulnerable and undergoing counseling.

Under the advice of Ron, my counselor, I wrote every traumatic event from my childhood into a journal. This was one of the hardest things I've ever had to do: remember the past and dig up every traumatic event that I had ever pushed deep down within me. As I wrote, I mourned and cried for the child I once was. I'd write a traumatic event and three more would follow. I wrote until I was physically and mentally exhausted and then dropped the journal into Ron's mailbox for his review before our next appointment. I also discussed at length the abuse I was enduring from my mother after the passing of my father. In this way, I was able to finally speak my truth and let go of the shame surrounding what had happened to me—the beatings and emotional and psychological abuse—in turn allowing myself to let go of the shame for what became unhealthy coping mechanisms.

In amazement, Ron held the trauma journal in his hand and told me it wasn't my fault; that I was a good person and that I should write a book. I knew it wasn't my fault, but I also knew that now, it was my own responsibility to heal. I read and researched the impact of trauma and healing trauma tirelessly so I could understand my parents and myself, and began putting these techniques into action in the effort to heal myself and my family once and for all; to end our generational trauma.

I also realized that my parents truly did the best they could, were good people, and had loved me the best they knew how. My life with my family wasn't all horrible: there was a balance of beauty, love, and laughter that ultimately allowed for forgiveness.

Through the techniques I was implementing for myself, such as mindfulness, future self journaling, listening to my body, staying present, understanding that my reactions of anxiety and anger came from a place of feeling physically and mentally attacked and unsafe in my own body, and yoga (to help regulate my nervous system), I found steady growth. However, self-sabotage and feelings of not being enough, not healing fast enough, not being capable of being loved, and not being deserving of love or compassion, would come into play almost every three months.

Indeed, a vital piece of my healing journey was missing: meditation. I rejected this idea with my arrogance and ego protecting me, telling myself over and over that I didn't need to become some Buddhist monk to heal. It was after Michael left—after we made our promise to one another to work on ourselves—that I finally soothed my ego into acknowledging what I needed, as much as it bucked and rejected it. Sure enough, through meditation, I went deeper into my own healing; it allowed me to understand that I didn't have to live in trauma any longer; to let go of the conditioning and patterns of my parents that were not mine to begin with and no longer served me; to return home to my authentic, true self.

After this awakening, I knew I had to share my story with others.

This was when Michael and I were awakened—truly, divinely, and spiritually. Ultimately, the Universe and God brought us back together to share our unconditional love story, and through reading many books, engaging in counseling, meditation, yoga, and journaling, and by hiring the best life coach out there, Heather Rine, we have come to meet our authentic selves again and are now living out our purpose. Endless love and gratitude to Heather; you are my Ambassador of Quan!

Within nine months of returning home to our authentic selves, I have become a real estate agent, left teaching to write and share my story, hired a writing manager, Jordan Wright, and begun working with Michael at our custom cabinetry business, Conde Design Group. I aspire to finish my book as soon as possible and to open my coaching business so that I can help to guide people who have experienced trauma like me; to show them that it truly is possible to come out the other side and become the best, most authentic version of yourself.

It now turns out that Michael and I were experiencing a spiritual awakening simultaneously, on our two separate journeys. Ultimately, our worlds collided once again in the form of unconditional love and forgiveness. I was sitting in church with Michael after many years of rejecting the notion of even setting foot in a church when the pastor said, "For those who are healed: serve." I repeated that back to myself. For those who are healed: serve. This was all the confirmation I needed: I knew I needed to get my story out.

Now, I know millions of others have stories of their own courageous battles—and my passion is to help them to tell it; to say it out loud; to move from fear to freedom and divine love through coaching. After learning so much in such a short amount of time, I desperately wanted to share it so I could heal my teenage daughters. I shared with them my new revelations and let them know that the awful, horrific parts of my childhood had been balanced with some really good parts. I explained the subconscious and conscious mind and shared that I had projected unhealed parts of myself onto them and saw them repeating some of these patterns of conditioning in their own lives. I wanted to instantly take away their pain.

Michael's daughter didn't want anything to do with either of us after we reunited; she had chosen to live with her mother and rejected the notion that Michael and I were healing—but Michael and I were ready to let go of the past and move forward. We truly understood the laws of the Universe; the power within each of us. We knew that everything we needed was inside us. We were now on a spiritual journey, no doubt about it. We also knew our daughters needed more healing and time. I still struggled in moments with my daughters, since I wanted more peace; more healing; more emotional regulation. I struggled with being misunderstood, since they offered a low level of compassion and empathy after I had struggled to give it to them for so long. My daughters would often threaten me with their choosing to live solely with their dad (we had shared custody), and would cross boundaries with disrespectful comments, curfews, alcohol-use, the time their guests were to leave, etc. They used the emotional blackmail that I had taught them on me. They were also repeating patterns of conditioning, emotional dysregulation, and an addiction to conflict and chaos that I had modeled their entire childhoods.

As a result of all of the above, I came to the true understanding in my heart that I needed to implement boundaries with my daughters in new ways to allow them to treat me and themselves with more respect and self-love. Hence, after the girls threatened to leave again, I let them go: they needed space and healing as much as I had before I'd commenced my self-healing journey.

While this was a very difficult decision, it led to the beginning of some honest communication between my ex-husband and I, and we began to explore forgiveness between the two of us. We put our egos aside and created a lifestyle that worked best for the girls, in turn building healthier, stronger relationships among us all. My daughters do not sleep at my house anymore; however, I see them and talk to them more now than I did when they were living with me. Something that could have turned out to be horrible shifted and became something beautiful. We are still growing and healing every day. I'm proud of that.

My dream is to become an inspirational coach, and in line with that, I'm looking to help clients to heal generational trauma; to move them on from surviving to thriving. I am taking on one client at a time.

I am currently a real estate agent, the co-owner (with my husband Michael) of Conde Design Group specializing in custom kitchens and interior design, an author (soon to be published), and, my most important job, a mom.

As a co-leader in our custom cabinet company, we inspire those who work for us and lead by example, instilling our belief in our employees. We listen, look at our actions and habits, create, change, and grow.

When it comes to working in the realm of healing others, I put into practice the notion of listening without judgement. There is something so incredibly powerful in this world about being able to listen to someone's story without sharing an opinion, only offering help once it's been asked of you. This is a skill that takes someone special to implement, as, in my own personal experience, people can project their opinions onto you without even realizing it. Throughout my life, the trauma I have experienced and the results of that trauma which I projected onto my own family has forced me to dig deep within myself and ask what it truly is that I am here to achieve. What is it that I needed to learn through everything that I experienced?

I truly believe that, while I know I need to share my story with as many people as possible, I'm also here to listen with an open heart and an open mind to others. All of my healing led me towards forgiveness and to understand the power it has over any situation—and the first step I made towards that forgiveness was when Ron, my counselor, took my journal that held every terrible, traumatic, and unhappy event in my life, looked me in the eye, and told me that I was a good person. The power of that moment shifted something within me, and I now want to be able to help shift that within others as well.

The relationship that I now have with my girls is one of open communication: we talk much more about deep, genuine topics than what we did when we were living together. I know that if I had had someone who I could have opened up to like this when I was growing up, it might not have taken me so long to heal; I may not have felt like I needed to hide my pain so deeply within me. I would have allowed myself to release the shame I felt because I felt like no one wanted to hear about what I was going through. I am now that person for others—and so my service to the community is a non-judgmental set of ears that is always ready to listen and show forgiveness to anyone who needs it. Everyone deserves that one basic need: to feel heard.

The more I share with people my own story, the more they open up to me—which is why I have decided to share my story with as many people as possible: to help give others the strength to share their own. There are so many people out there who have experienced trauma on all different levels, and I truly believe that the more people share their stories, the less stigma there will be around it and the more people will be able to come forward and talk about what they have been through without the fear of being gaslighted. You never know who you might impact, so share, share, share. My story might impact someone in a way that might shift their life for the better, and so may yours—but you'll never know if you keep it to yourself!

The key highlights of my journey have been absolute gratitude: I never believed that everything I had experienced would lead me to this point, especially since I believed I was thriving when really, I was only surviving. I am so proud of myself for learning to see my actions in a new light and for taking that step back to see how my own actions were impacting my life instead of fighting with myself and continuing to blame others. Not only was this the catalyst for my self-love and self-compassion, but it also completely shifted my relationships in my life: I never had genuinely healthy relationships with anyone before I started on this journey. Now, I know what not only I, but my family and friends, deserve, and I am so proud of myself for figuring that out and implementing boundaries within my life that have forced me to keep these healthy relationships in place, with room to grow.

While this may not seem like much to people who haven't been in this position before, for me, knowing that I am able to break the generational trauma that I grew up in so that my daughters don't suffer (and their children don't suffer) is something that means more to me than I could ever put into coherent words. My "normal" life now is one of such happiness that I sometimes can't even begin to imagine that I believed what I experienced before was normal. Knowing that I am able to step into a place of gratitude and acknowledge that everything is happening for me and not to me has opened me up to so much goodness in my life: before, anytime anything started to go south, my mind immediately began seeking out someone to blame to push the problem onto so I didn't have to face my own demons. But now, I actually look forward to digging deeper within myself with awareness and interest so I can see how I can grow. I know that there is so much more of me left to uncover, after all-and how exciting is that?

To you, my reader, I offer you unconditional love. I believe that every person that walks this earth is divinely connected to something greater; I believe in self-healing in the sense that you have the capability to heal no matter what your circumstances are. I leave you with the resources I have used to get me to the quantum leaps I have made. These are books that I have read (and still refer to often as my guides)—and I am also sharing with you the names of the people who have helped me through my awakening and the techniques I use today. There are a variety of resources out there, and some might speak louder to you than others. The books are listed in the order I read them.

- *Creating the Champion Within* by Molly Kennedy.
- *Out of the Fog: Moving from Confusion to Clarity After Narcissistic Abuse* by Dana Morningstar.
- *The Body Keeps the Score: Brain, Mind, and Body in the Healing of Trauma* by Bessel Van Der Kolk, M.D.
- *How To Do The Work* by Dr. Nicole LePera (she can also be found on Facebook,
- Instagram, and YouTube under The Holistic Psychologist).
- Sonia Ricotti's Unsinkable Course.
- My coach Heather Rine (a consultant for Thinking Into Results, a program for leaders, developed from the Bob Proctor and Sandy Gallagher Institute) and also the founder of Quantum ED-U.
- Oliver The Spiritual Activator (found on Instagram, Facebook, and YouTube).
- Chanel Mulcahy's virtual one-to-one group, corporate breathwork, sound healing (my personal favorite), and coaching (can be found on Instagram).
- Dr. Joe Despenza (New York Times bestselling author and the king of meditation, who can be found on Facebook, Instagram, and YouTube).
- Reverend Michael Beckwith (Facebook and Instagram).

- *The Secret* by Rhonda Byrne (Netflix and Amazon Prime).
- Finding Joe (YouTube).

On top of these mediums, I also work with clients one at a time so I can give you the honor of my full attention and time. When we work together, I go through everything I did to further enhance and continue my healing and growth in great detail. I know that each situation is different and that every person who is going through this journey will have different needs—which is why I work with one client at a time, one-on-one, as there is no "one size fits all" approach in this journey.

Alternatively, should you simply like to stay in my life and feel heard, you can reach out to me at YourValor17@gmail.com. I would love to let you know that you matter, like someone else did for me; I know there is something incredibly powerful about having someone just listen to you, and I am here to let you know that I would be honored to be that person for you!

If I could leave you with one last bit of information before you leave me for today, it's this: you are in control, even when you don't feel like you are. Every part of this journey you're on is there to push you into becoming the truest, most authentic version of yourself. You are perfect in your current space, and you will still be perfect when you heal.

You are a good person.

Contact Denise

 truetoself17@gmail.com

HAYLEY PAIGE

**Founder & CEO of Onyx Publishing, Book
Mentor and Ghostwriter**

ONCE UPON A TIME, there was a little girl.
At first glance, she was nothing special; just a
peasant girl. But she was intelligent and driven;
kind and considerate.

She loved school and friends; animals and nature;
but above all, her joy came from books—both reading
and creating, turning pages beneath the moon's light.

She would spend hours and hours immersed in the
pages of fairytales, imagining her own adventures that
were yet to come and thinking about the day when she

would open her own publishing house and send stories out across the land.

However, things soon got difficult for the peasant girl, and so she decided she would start a new life in a land far far away.

It was there that she met a handsome prince—a prince who showed her patience and kindness; who gave her gifts of jewels and promises of devotion and happiness.

He seemed to be everything she had hoped she would someday find, but he told her that, in order for them to live Happily Ever After, she would need to build her castle as high as could be to keep all the witches, dragons, and ogres out.

He told her she should change her hair (because princesses don't have mouse-brown hair), and that would make him love her more.

He told her to dress so that none of the ogres in other lands would be tempted to steal her away.

He told her to always be grateful that she had him because he was the handsome prince of fairytales, and it was down to pure luck she'd even managed to snare him.

And he told her not to tell anyone if he hit her, because it was her fault, after all, and he wouldn't want her to be embarrassed.

And so the now-princess sat in her tall castle,

keeping the witches, dragons, and ogres out, bent over the straw she was spinning into gold for the handsome prince.

Her hair jet-black.

Her feminine wiles hidden.

Her eyes looking down.

Because she could not stand to lose what she had found; what she believed she did not deserve to have.

Even if it did mean she soon forgot about books and adventure; her friends and animals; nature and happiness.

Even if it did mean a life focused on survival.

Survival in the wake of broken wrists and ear bones.

Strangulation and sustained beatings.

Head-blows, amnesia, and PTSD.

This was the survival of a princess who was ruining her own Happily Ever After.

Who, little to her knowledge at the time, was recreating the life she had so often dreamt of escaping when she had been just a peasant girl who had sought refuge in books.

A girl whose sunshine had been stolen by those who were supposed to love and protect her the most.

Whose should-be confidantes shunned her for disclosing the nights of darkness and fear at the hands of those people.

A girl who lived in a home of secrecy and shame; fear and repression.

One day, after years of living in her castle spinning gold, the princess looked up from her spindle and glanced over at the handsome prince...

And suddenly she realized: all this time he had been wearing a disguise and was, in fact, an ogre himself!

The princess was shocked. She sat for a moment, remembering everything he had told her, everything he'd done, and like magic, the clouds parted...

A spectrum of dazzling light flashed through the arched windows, and soon everything became clear...

She had been keeping the good out and the evil within her walls!

And so, when the ogre wasn't around, she called high from her topmost tower and sought the help of old friends.

One who could find another castle, far far away.

One who could weave blankets.

One who could watch over her as she slept.

And then, one cold night in the thick of winter, she escaped.

And do you know, she went on to live an incredibly happy life...

That peasant girl opened a publishing house, where she spent the days sharing others' stories, far and wide across the lands, helping them to build their castles in the sky.

And, after years spent healing her heart and spinning gold for her own joy, she met a real prince; one who loved every version of her, whatever that looked like.

Sometimes, the peasant girl can be heard telling people how, once upon a time, she'd known a princess who was nearly killed by an ogre, but that the princess had found her inner strength, recognized her worth, started a new life, and followed her dreams...

And then she can be seen smiling as she watches her story inspire others to embrace, write and share their own, and live their own Happily Ever After ending.

*

In the spring of 2021, I posted the above fairytale story to one of my social media platforms. I can't say for sure what inspired me in that very moment to strip myself bare of the professional, always-put-together mask and share with the world this incredibly vulnerable, albeit small fragment of my experience with domestic violence, but my story, laced in an otherworldly, easy-to-digest narrative, set in motion an incredible sequence of events and further echoed one of my core beliefs:

Your story has an incredible power.

Of course, I have always known this to be true, but I've also known there are different levels of knowing: there is the knowing we have when we simply believe something to be true without ever having experienced it—a knowing that is fluid and which finds itself changed when situations arise and make themselves a home in our lives; and then, on the other side of the mirror, is the knowing that is ingrained deep in our soul, which comes only as a result of our truly seeing, feeling, tasting, and journeying through a given moment.

As a little girl, the power of story was a knowing in my mind and heart; it was something I felt at a level that derived from reading; from seeing the world and its joys and pains through another's eyes. It was this level of understanding, coupled with a pure love for books—not just the reading experience, but the tangible, beautiful thing that is a book (worlds inscribed on pages, and bound and wrapped in beautiful covers)—that led me to aspire, at just six years old, to someday own my own publishing house. But of course, at thirty-eight years old and almost a decade after launching that very same publishing house, my knowing is so very different.

And that knowing was born directly after my posting of my domestic violence fairytale at thirty-seven.

Other areas of my knowing were derived from an entire spectrum of experience, from bliss all the way through to torturous agony. It is the culmination of these experiences, each so full of color and packed with lessons and learnings, that has led me down a path of Survivor to Thriver. So many of these areas of real, lived, closer-than-you-can-bear experiences I never expected to have touch my life, but they have forced their way in and opened my eyes to a whole other level of human experience, compassion, and understanding that can't possibly be wished away regardless.

Experiences such as childhood trauma and abuse.

Chronic sickness.

Eating disorders.

Sexual abuse.

Family breakdown and homelessness.

Grooming.

Sexual assault.

Domestic violence.

Miscarriage.

PTSD.

Anterograde amnesia.

And domestic violence and abuse trials.

Each of these traumas-turned-blessings have contributed to the beautiful life I have painstakingly built and lovingly nurtured. And it is this—the choice to take a trauma and mindfully pull lessons and value from it, coupled with a very conscious appreciation of all I have and explicit statements of gratitude in all things—that formed my first step into Thriving.

It is this step that I feel is probably the most important of them all.

Of course, it can sometimes feel difficult to show appreciation, especially in the dark times, but I know from my own journey that there is always joy to be found in life, no matter the circumstance or situation. I say this from a very experienced standpoint, without rose-tinted glasses or any jaded perspective.

To provide some context, in 2016, I found myself in one of the most painful, unexpected, confusing, frightening, and awful situations—the worst of my life without exception. Here, in the space of a day, I went from being happy and generally quite content to living in a nightmare. And although this part of my story is not mine to share (and so the details can be spared), what I will say is that myself and my daughters laughed every single day and still actively filled our time with as much happiness and gratitude as we possibly could. There is something remarkably freeing about being able to laugh and live in the moment when tragedy has not only arrived on your doorstep but driven a hole through the very brickwork of your life. To take those moments and truly bask in their light proves that, no matter the obstacle or twist in the road, it is truly possible to choose to Thrive.

The second step—and arguably one of the most pivotal on this journey from Surviving to Thriving—was *choosing more*.

My moment of not only choosing more, but realizing and fully absorbing that I deserved it, was November 2012. I was sat working in my office in the most beautiful French chateau, my eldest daughter next to me while my eight-month-old baby girl slept in one of the five bedrooms, my violent husband gaming in the lounge. As the one responsible for earning the money and maintaining our life in France, I was working late in pursuit of a deadline and the pressure was on.

Despite almost killing me eighteen months before and narrowly escaping prison, my husband had shown no sign of reform, the only changes in his behavior being a significant worsening in his treatment of me. In the eight months since our daughter had been born, he had taken his violence from one extreme to another, my life becoming nothing more than an endless battle of survival and a constant wondering of when he would eventually succeed in beating me to death and leaving my children motherless and in his care. My only respite came in the times he would fly back to England to be with his friends—men fifteen years younger than he—which, thankfully, he would do often. During these times, my daughters and I would fill the house with as much laughter and happiness as we possibly could.

On this particular night, however, while in the thick of editing a PhD thesis, I heard my husband walking up the stairs. Glancing to my eldest daughter and smiling with feigned reassurance, I turned back to my screen and tried to resume work, my heart pounding as I wondered whether Dr. Jekyll or Mr. Hyde would be making his appearance.

I don't fully remember the details of what happened then, in that moment, but my husband entered the office, aggression and volatility ever-present. I remember feeling panicked—fight-or-flight kicking in—and wondering what was going to happen. And although what unfolded remains hazy, what I do remember are these words:

"Get this through your thick fucking skull..."

I remember looking at this man, this disgusting human being I had once loved, and being acutely aware of my daughter's presence. I remember acknowledging that this man thought it was okay to speak to me like that, in front of my daughter, and that he had a complete disregard for how he was frightening her, a nine-year-old little girl, not to mention the presence of our baby just a few rooms away.

And then, like the straw that broke the camel's back, I thought to myself, *That's your husband! Your husband thinks it's acceptable to speak to you like that! No more.*

Right then and there, I realized I deserved more. I looked at him as he continued to spit venom—words that could make a grown man's ears bleed—and chose to pursue more, for myself and, most importantly, my daughters.

When his tirade was over and he had left the room, I told my daughter this was it, enough was enough, and that we would be leaving. I promised her a life of safety and happiness, far away from his grasp. No more surviving. I would choose to thrive. And then I never looked back.

I wish I could say it was easy, but the period spent breaking away was not without its difficulties; however, words simply can't do justice to the feeling of safety we enjoyed as we slowly but surely removed the shackles and built a life free from violence, complete with the long-imagined publishing house, which I launched in the first few months of my freedom.

This process leads very nicely to the third step in moving from Survivor to Thriver—healing—which was both a terribly long and miraculously short journey:

It was long, because of the years spent being pushed

from pillar to post, and wasting my energy and tears on talking therapies with a countless number of counsellors; approaches that did nothing but delay my healing and forced me to revisit memories I wanted to keep buried—and all without any real peace or calm at the end of any session.

But then it was miraculously short, because, in the late spring of 2021, I found myself in a mentoring container with a truly incredible human being with the most amazing neurolinguistic programming superpower. In just three hours, he helped me to work my way through decades worth of trauma, pain, and anguish, and emerge from the other side anxiety-free and feeling worthy and loveable. And although I felt like I had been thriving for a few years before this moment of pure weightlessness, there was definitely a turning point with the revelation that nothing that has ever happened to me before matters now.

And then, the final step: breaking free from any gags and those who wish to silence me.

It isn't without its own irony and difficulties that I, a creator of books, facilitator of storytelling and advocate for documenting journeys, has always felt unable to openly discuss her own history—the difficulties and traumas and the people responsible—until this very recent time. It has felt almost counterintuitive for me to shroud in secrecy so many of the dark moments that have etched themselves in my memory as the key reference points in my life. I believe that who I am—she who is without the fear of others' opinions, voices, and toxic behaviors—is someone unashamedly honest and open, no matter the fallout. And although I've told snippets of my story to those I've trusted, for most of my life—right from being a toddler—I have allowed others to tell me what I should and shouldn't do, what I am and am not allowed to say, and what secrets I can and cannot share.

Even many of the adults around me mirrored this behavior, only showing certain areas of our life to the people we were supposedly close to—and that birthed in me a feeling that I had to be careful what I shared and my reasons for so doing. From being a young child to now, I have always sought refuge in words—whether in the form of books or conversations with close ones—to sort through the complex headspaces and circumstances I have found myself in, and yet, during my childhood, many facets of our life as a family were veiled in secrecy. From small matters, such as my parentage (my mother insisted I never tell anybody that my stepfather was not my biological father—a wish I put down to her own embarrassment over our family dynamics and having had children with different men), to much bigger problems, such as the root cause of my chronic vomiting from five years of age (the result of the abuse and stress I endured from my stepfather, but that my mother refused to get me help for, apparently for fear of Social Services becoming involved) and the sexual abuse I endured from my older brother at ten years old (a matter I was firmly told by my mother I was not to disclose to anybody after his being sent to care), there was a long list of things I was not to share with anyone outside of our home.

And all of this while being raised to be honest, tell the truth, and never lie.

The need to fall silent felt, at times, like it could choke me. My natural instinct was to talk, to start from A and make sense of everything all the way through to Z, and I felt an ever-pressing need to confide in people. However, my mother often said I had a tendency to "land [her] in it", and so I consciously made every effort to skip over certain parts with the aim of protecting myself and those in my immediate circle.

Hence, when my Year 5 teacher took me to the side one afternoon and asked me if everything was okay at home and stressed that I could always talk to her no matter what, I simply shrugged and heard my ten-year-old self tell her everything was fine.

With a multitude of secrets spanning every area of

my life, right from being a toddler, it is then no wonder that, as I experienced more and more trauma, I chose to drape it in secrecy, feeling a combination of shame at my reality and fear at what would happen if I spoke up; fear of consequences, threats, and losing those I treasured if they didn't believe what I said.

Essentially, I was scared of the truth and its power, and the kind of hot water I could find myself in as a result.

This meant that, when I found myself at the beginning of my horrifically violent relationship at twenty-four years old, I kept much of what was happening to myself. Although I occasionally confided in my sisters and mother, I quickly realized that, not only would I be in more serious trouble for doing so, but I also couldn't rely on anyone to help me escape. As such, for the most part, I opted for deceit through omission. This meant that, when my husband asked me if I'd told anyone about what he'd recently done, I could quite honestly say no.

It was only at certain times, when things got darker than usual and I genuinely feared for my life, that I would share snippets of information with those around me. However, nothing much was ever done to help, and I found that my disclosing of events elicited reactions that hurt me more deeply than the physical violence: in January 2011, for example, after my husband strangled me on our kitchen table, taking me to the point of losing consciousness and subsequently causing me to miscarry, my mother asked me, "What are you doing to wind him up?"

Similarly, when my husband subjected me to a sustained attack that very nearly killed me and left my then-seven-year-old daughter without a mother, my dad, when I asked him why he hadn't come to the hospital or done anything about the situation, stated that he "hadn't been very happy about it".

And when I revealed to my mother that I hadn't, in fact, tripped up the stairs and broken my wrist, but that my husband had been responsible, she focused on the lie and said she was "disappointed" in me for being so deceitful.

As a result, a whole spectrum of horror went untold, with only the walls inside my home able to tell the stories—a situation indeed very reminiscent of my childhood situation, which also harbored the same "don't ask, don't tell" culture.

Stories of how I was pulled out of bed and dragged downstairs by my hair in the thick of night.

How I went through ordeals so horrifying I thought I'd be killed while my daughters sat downstairs, one five months old and swinging in her baby swing.

And how the abuse and beatings were so bad I

developed anterograde amnesia that ultimately led me to struggle to recall a multitude of events years later, both related to the abuse and not.

With so much more stretching right back to the earliest years of my childhood.

Now, I accept and embrace all that has happened and what I have managed to pull from every single experience. Now I know my truth is my truth, and I welcome and appreciate the ways in which it has shaped me.

And nobody will ever silence me again.

However, as much as there is tremendous power to be found in sharing one's story, there is also a very real fear of sharing—and between these spaces of fear and power is a bridge to be navigated; a bridge with many steppingstones.

First, there needs to be the recognition that anyone trying to silence you has their own demons to battle. What is it they don't want you to share? Is it because it will make them look bad? Is it because they don't want to be faced with the reality of what they've done and how you feel about it?

Second, ask yourself how you would feel if *you* read your story, but someone else has written it. Would you be judgmental, cynical, non-believing? Would you question the narrative? Or would you reach out to the author and offer warmth, appreciation, and gratitude? Remember, only those offering a safe space are worthy of your time and energy.

And third, if the sharing of your story could empower another human being, make them feel heard, show them they're not alone, or otherwise just shape their existence for the better, wouldn't it be a disservice not to share it? Your story is your own, and you have every right to share it, especially if you can take what you've learnt and help someone on their journey.

For me, sharing my story has allowed me to truly embrace all facets of who I am, who I've been, and the work it's taken to get me here—and that has involved me sharing those experiences with those around me, the good *and* the bad.

It has also proven to be incredibly enlightening, and showed me who is truly there for me and who has my best interests at heart. Similarly, it has directed a spotlight onto those who explicitly told me not to write my story, my mother being one such person. Funnily enough, this allowed for even greater clarity and a well-lit pathway when I ultimately chose to continue with my plan, because, without question, nobody should ever be silenced.

Providing a tiny glimpse into the crystal ball of my truth has shaped both my personal and professional life, and led to incredibly empowering, freeing realizations (which can act as affirmations for anyone wanting to write their book):

- I absolutely should share my story; the good, the bad, the ugly—warts and all. It's *my* story, after all!
- *My* people (my tribe; the ones who truly care and who embrace me for all I am) will listen and, more importantly, will *hear*.
- There is no shame in my truth (and only those who are scared of you sharing their wrongs will seek to gag you).
- If someone has wronged me and they're scared of the voice they've forced me to develop, that is everything to do with them and nothing to do with me.
- If my journey has allowed me to travel from Survivor to Thriver, there is nothing to do but embrace every curve, moment, hurt, and opportunity for growth.

My sharing created something so powerful and almost magical; it not only allowed me to feel heard and be seen, but it also empowered other women to share *their* truth; to disclose details of what they have experienced and what ultimately encouraged them to build a life focused on thriving.

And it is this truly being seen and heard that can prove to be so life-affirming.

We all know looks can be deceiving.

We all know nobody knows what really goes on behind closed doors.

And yet we all live our lives without real acknowledgement of these facts.

We still assume social media provides a realistic snapshot of someone's life.

We still believe that the fact they *look* happy means they truly *are* happy.

And most of us don't even stop to conceive of the possibility that all might not be quite as it seems.

Everybody has a story to tell, and a person's story tells the tale of their journey; of their truth, with its own twists and turns and the lens through which they choose to tell it. It is the combination of story and lens that forms a person's truth; a truth that may very well differ from another person who endured the very same journey.

The form this truth takes can depend on all sorts of elements—vantage point, the sides of the situation visible to a person or their degree of involvement, and where the storyteller ultimately stands, both in consideration of the milestones that act as their key points of reference and with hindsight as their friend.

The fact is this: your story is your own, and nobody can ever tell you how to interpret or feel about what you experienced.

I, for one, am so glad I shared my experience: my sharing led to the birth of this very publication—*Powerhouse Women: Survivor to Thriver*—and gave courage to dozens of women behind an influx of emails, social media comments, and personal messages who had also experienced their own horrors of abuse.

When we tell our story, we open up our soul and invite readers into our truth. This is the most important aspect to acknowledge when we tell our story: it doesn't matter who wants to debate the facts or say things didn't happen quite like that; *our journey is our own*; it's *our* truth. It's told through the lens we view it with consideration to the facts we hold, and just because someone on the outside isn't in possession of the whole truth, the ugly bones of it, doesn't mean the ugliness isn't there.

I've come to learn that nobody can be blamed for thinking a situation was different to how it actually was if they've only been shown a small glimmer of insight. If Little Red Riding Hood pulled back the cloth on just half of her basket to reveal delicious fresh jams, scones, and breads, an unsuspecting grandmother could be forgiven for thinking the basket was full of the same—but that doesn't mean Little Red Riding Hood is leading her grandmother astray if it materializes that the Big Bad Wolf ravaged half of its contents when she momentarily strayed from her path.

My only trouble comes from the grandmothers who continue to state the basket was full-to-bursting with satisfying goodies, long after watching the wolf help himself.

*

Should you feel compelled to share *your* story—your truth—the peasant-girl-turned-publisher can be booked for a no-pressure preliminary conversation if you'd like to discuss getting your book blueprinted, written, and published so that you can attract in all the land has to offer and build your very own castle, full of light.

You can also help yourself to free book-planning treats via the links below.

Ogres need not apply.

Contact Hayley

 www.onyxpublishing.com

 www.hayleypaigeinternational.com

 www.facebook.com/hayleypaige222

 www.facebook.com/groups/booktobooked

 HayleyPaigeInternational

Hayley's Resources

Book-Writing and -Publishing Discovery Call:
www.calendly.com/onyxpublishing/discovery

Free Blueprinting Training:
www.hayleypaigeinternational.com